BrightRED Study Guide

CfE HIGHER

ADMINISTRATION and IT

William Reynolds and Jane Sturrock

BrightRED
PUBLISHING

First published in 2016 by:
Bright Red Publishing Ltd
1 Torphichen Street
Edinburgh
EH3 8HX

MIX
Paper from
responsible sources
FSC® C013254

A CIP record for this book is available from the British Library

ISBN 978-1-906736-77-4

With thanks to:
PDQ Digital Media Solutions Ltd (layout) and Anna Stevenson (edit)

Cover design and series book design by Caleb Rutherford – e i d e t i c

Acknowledgements
Every effort has been made to seek all copyright holders. If any have been overlooked, then Bright Red Publishing will be delighted to make the necessary arrangements.

Permission has been sought from all relevant copyright holders and Bright Red Publishing are grateful for the use of the following:
eelnosiva/iStock.com (p 6); Ridofranz/iStock.com (p 13); Viktor_Gladkov/iStock.com (p 30); fotek/iStock.com (p80); CreativeImages/iStock.com (p 89); maselkoo99/iStock.com (p 89); Norasit Kaewsai/iStock.com (p 90); ragsac/iStock.com (p 92); Rawpixel Ltd/iStock.com (p 96); Buzya_Kalapkina/iStock.com (p 96); AlexanderMas/iStock.com (p 98); Orla/iStock.com (p 98); Lpstudio/iStock.com (p 98); shironosov/iStock.com (p 100); gehringj/iStock.com (p 100); monkeybusinessimages/iStock.com (p 101); The poster 'Health and Safety Law: what you need to know' is reproduced by permission of the Health and Safety Executive (p 102); jfmdesign/iStock.com (p 103); gradts/iStock.com (p 104); The HSE logo is reproduced by permission of the Health and Safety Executive (p 105); monkeybusinessimages/iStock.com (p 108); Ibrakovic/iStock.com (p 108); RakicN/iStock.com (p 109); russwitherington1/iStock.com (p 111); The case study 'Working from home' by Martin Catchpole, reproduced by permission of Arise Virtual Solutions (p 111); nickylarson974/iStock.com (p 113); hjalmeida/iStock.com (p 114); scanrail/iStock.com (p 118); Model-la/iStock.com (p 118); Pavel Hlystov/iStock.com (p 118); lenscap67/iStock.com (p 120); Jirsak/iStock.com (p 122); 4774344sean/iStock.com (p 123); chany167/iStock.com (p 124); Jag_cz/Shutterstock.com (p 125); Tesco Plc (p 125); Prykhodov/iStock.com (p 126); McDonald's case study, reproduced by permission of McDonald's Restaurants Limited (p 127); Screenshots used with permission from Microsoft.

Printed and bound in the UK by Martins the Printers.

CONTENTS

INTRODUCTION

INTRODUCING HIGHER ADMINISTRATION AND IT

THE IMPORTANCE OF ADMINISTRATION

A successful business needs knowledgeable and highly-skilled administrators who can provide high-level administrative support to ensure the smooth and efficient running of the organisation.

An Administrative Assistant has to manage the day-to-day operations of an office. This could range from undertaking basic routine tasks to taking responsibility at a more senior level and overseeing the work of junior staff; this is all dependent on the size and structure of the organisation. Administrative support could therefore involve keyboarding, reading and replying to e-mails, composing letters and memoranda, supervising staff (including planning their work assignments), customer care, dealing with confidential matters (staff-related or otherwise), writing reports, organising meetings, implementing and developing organisational policies and procedures, project management and Health and Safety.

Breakthrough developments in information technology (IT) and the increased use of emerging technologies have had a major impact on the way many administrative tasks are undertaken and indeed in the way organisations function and communicate. As office automation and the use of IT to execute various office procedures continues to develop, there will be an increased need for skilled Administrative Assistants.

This Higher Study Guide will help develop your knowledge and understanding of the role Administrative Assistants play in modern business organisations. Practical activities will also help you develop the IT skills necessary to organise, analyse, store, and present and communicate business information using appropriate software applications. This guide will also help you to develop and apply skills for learning, skills for work and skills for life.

HIGHER COURSE CONTENT

The Higher course contains three units of study:

Administrative theory and practice

This unit enables you to develop an in-depth knowledge and understanding of administration in, and the impact of IT on, the workplace. You will acquire an in-depth knowledge and understanding of the factors contributing to the effectiveness of the administrative function, such as efficient time and task management, complying with workplace legislation, successful teams, organising effective meetings and good customer care.

IT solutions for administrators

The purpose of this unit is to develop learners' skills in IT and in the organisation and management of information in administration-related contexts. Learners will develop the ability to utilise a range of functions within IT applications covering word processing, spreadsheets and databases, and to use them to analyse, process and manage information in order to create and edit relatively complex business documents. This unit, in particular, will be supported with a range of tasks on the Digital Zone to allow learners to confidently develop and apply their ICT skills at an advanced level.

Communication in administration

The purpose of this unit is to enable learners to develop a range of IT skills (focusing particularly on presentation software) for researching and communicating complex information to others. This will enable learners to communicate information, taking account of the needs of the audience. Learners will develop an understanding of barriers

contd

to communication and ways of overcoming them to ensure communication is understood. This unit will also develop learners' knowledge and understanding of how to maintain the security and confidentiality of information.

COURSE ASSESSMENT - INTERNAL ASSESSMENT

Each of the three units above has a formal unit assessment. Unit assessments can be undertaken on a unit-by-unit basis or by a combined assessment. All units will be marked by the classroom teacher as a pass or fail. However, SQA will undertake external quality assurance (external verification) to ensure assessments are marked consistently and meet national standards.

COURSE ASSESSMENT - EXTERNAL ASSESSMENT

Theory question paper

The question paper is worth 30 marks (30 per cent of the total mark). The question paper consists of two sections:

- **Section 1** – This section has 10 marks and consists of a set of mandatory questions based on a given stimulus. The questions can come from any areas covered in the course.
- **Section 2** – This section has 20 marks and consists of mandatory questions. Questions from each section of the course will be sampled, ensuring there is a balanced coverage across the course.

The question paper is set and marked by SQA. Learners will complete this in one hour. A specimen examination paper is available to learners in the Digital Zone.

Practical assignment

The purpose of this is to address challenge and application. It assesses your ability to apply problem-solving and advanced IT skills in the context of a complex scenario.

This assignment is set by SQA on an annual basis and conducted under a high degree of supervision and control within presenting centres. You will complete the assignment in two hours. The assignment is worth 70 marks (70 per cent of the total mark).

To secure an overall award in Administration and IT at Higher Grade, you must achieve all three unit assessments as well as securing a pass in the external course assessments.

EXAMINATION HINTS - QUESTION PAPER

Before you start answering questions in the external examination paper, you should identify the key 'command word' used in each question. This will ensure that you tailor your response to the demands of the question being asked. The table below outlines the key command words which could be used in the final external examination.

COMMAND WORD	MEANING
State	Listing or bullet points would be acceptable here.
Suggest	More than just naming or stating. Put forward a recommendation or advise on a possible course of action.
Outline	Identify key features and provide a brief description where appropriate.
Describe	Give a description and use examples where possible as part of the description.
Explain	Give a definition and then an example as to how something may or may not be affected.
Discuss	Give advantages and disadvantages where possible. Use examples to expand your answer, and if possible give a conclusion to your answer.
Compare	You must be able to compare the similarities or differences between the items, again giving a conclusion if necessary. A key word that you can use in this type of question is 'whereas'.
Justify	You must be able to give reasons why a certain course of action is being taken.
Implications	You should be able to state what the likely outcome of a particular action will be in the longer term, either on a person or on an organisation.
Consequences	You must be able to identify the initial impact of the action being followed.

INTRODUCTION

COMMUNICATION IN BUSINESS

Communication is vital within an organisation: everyone in an organisation needs to communicate effectively with each other as well as with customers. When choosing a communication method, you should think about the relationship between sender and receiver, and how quickly the information has to be passed on. Whatever method of communication is chosen, it is very important that information is kept secure at all times.

VIDEO LINK

Go to www.brightredbooks.net and watch the video – it offers seven tips for effective communication.

DON'T FORGET

Internal communication is communication between people in the same organisation. Good internal communication is important so that work flows clearly and correctly and so the right people receive the right information at the right time. This communication tends to be more informal as you already know your colleagues.

DON'T FORGET

External communication is with customers, suppliers or anyone else outside the business. External communication is very important as it helps create a good impression. This communication needs to be more formal.

METHODS OF COMMUNICATION

Method	Description
Face-to-face (e.g. a meeting, an interview, a conversation with a colleague/customer)	Used if immediate feedback is required and also if any uncertainties need to be clarified. With face-to-face communication you are able to gauge body language and facial expressions.
Oral (e.g. telephone call)	Used when a quick answer is required. Lots of organisations use this as their main method of communication – particularly since the increase in use of mobile phones and smartphones. It is convenient and allows for two-way communication so clarification can be provided if necessary.
Written (e.g. letters, memoranda/reports in printed format)	Still very popular in business, this type of communication provides a permanent record that can be kept for future reference. It also allows people time to read and understand what is being communicated.
Electronic (e.g. intranet, internet, e-mail, blogs or social networking)	Nowadays, using technology to communicate electronically is one of the most common ways of sending and receiving information. It allows information to be passed on immediately and enables people to communicate 24/7.
Visual (e.g. PowerPoint presentations)	This can be an effective way of communicating complex information to groups of staff. Pictures, graphs, sound and different formats can be used to effectively grab listeners' attention.

Written or oral?

WRITTEN COMMUNICATION	
ADVANTAGES	**DISADVANTAGES**
Provides a permanent record for the future.	Can take longer to prepare and send.
Can be more structured and consistent.	Inflexible – there is no immediate feedback or interaction.
If there are many points to be covered, it is better to write them down.	Sender cannot use non-verbal cues, such as body language.
Written communication can be looked at when it is convenient.	Some people may be unable to access it easily, e.g. people with dyslexia.

ORAL COMMUNICATION	
ADVANTAGES	**DISADVANTAGES**
Information can be given faster than written communication.	Distractions and interruptions can interfere.
Easy to direct to the desired person.	Personalities and emotions can create a barrier.
Can be cheaper than writing/using technology.	Can be difficult to control, especially with large numbers of people.
Allows for two-way discussion/interaction.	Number of participants may be limited.
Instant feedback – person receiving the information can ask questions.	Not as structured or consistent.
Face-to-face interaction gives indication of response through non-verbal cues.	No permanent record – information can be forgotten or people can disagree about what was said.
Message can be changed if the person has not understood what you have been trying to communicate.	
Appropriate for personal messages and delicate situations.	

BARRIERS TO EFFECTIVE COMMUNICATION

Communication is often ineffective; for example, if two people are unable to express themselves in the same language, a barrier will be created. By being aware of the factors that can cause problems in communication, you can minimise their effect. Other barriers to communication are:

- **Distortion** – If the message is not accurately stated, jargon is used or the receiver does not correctly interpret the message.
- **Noise**
  - physical – traffic, roadworks, machinery
  - technical – bad connection, faulty line
  - social – clash of personalities
  - psychological – excessive emotion interfering
- **Differences in perception** – People of different ages, cultures or educational backgrounds or those with contrasting personalities interpret situations differently.
- **Jumping to conclusions** – Hearing or seeing what you expect rather than the actual message.
- **Lack of interest** – The receiver doesn't engage with the message so the meaning is lost.
- **Information overload** – Too much information can make the recipient tired and confused.
- **Bias and selectivity** – You only receive part of the message as you filter out the rest. For example, if you are told 'You're doing a good job but need more training', you may subconsciously choose to hear only the first part of what has been said.
- **Lack of feedback** – If a message is sent and there is no response, you cannot be sure that the message has been received or understood.

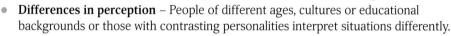

DON'T FORGET

Poor communication can impact on individual members of staff and the business as a whole.

The effects of poor communication

ON THE INDIVIDUAL EMPLOYEE	ON THE BUSINESS ORGANISATION
Poor staff performance: staff may be unsure of instructions they have received or how to ask for help.	Poor communication may lead to poor decision-making.
Damaged working relationships due to errors and disagreements with colleagues.	Lowered productivity and increased costs.
Stress caused by frustration.	Poor relationships with customers and suppliers could lead to a fall in sales and profits.
Low morale and low self-confidence.	Increased staff turnover: good staff may leave and it takes time and money to find suitable replacements.

THE ADMINISTRATIVE ASSISTANT

The Administrative Assistant must ensure that all communication is as effective as possible. The following principles should always be considered:

Accurate	The information transmitted should be accurate – correct and true.
Complete	The information must be complete with no key facts missing. A message that is only partly communicated will be misunderstood.
Timely	The timing of the message is important. The information must be delivered on time and should be up-to-date.
Relevant	Good communication is adapted to meet the needs of the audience. Will the audience be interested in what you are telling them? Do they need to know it? Will it be useful to them?
Cost-effective	Preparing to communicate takes time and money. Information has to be gathered and collated for delivery. Time is money in business and the cost of communicating should not be more than the benefit the communication brings.
Meaningful	Use suitable language and the most appropriate method. Will the audience find the information easy to understand? Think about the age and size of your audience.

It is also important that, when communicating, the Administrative Assistant follows organisational procedures in relation to data handling legislation.

 THINGS TO DO AND THINK ABOUT

1 Outline the five main methods that can be used to communicate information and give an example where it would be appropriate to use each method.
2 Describe three barriers to effective communication.
3 Describe two effects of poor communication between a departmental manager and a member of staff.
4 Outline the advantages of using PowerPoint to communicate with staff.
5 Explain the difference between internal and external communication.

 ONLINE TEST

Test yourself on this topic at www.brightredbooks.net

EDITING A PRESENTATION

PowerPoint is software that uses slides to create and build dynamic **slide presentations** that can include text, bulleted lists, images, charts, animation, narration, images and video. You can add as many slides as you want to a presentation and you can view or play back your presentation at any time. You can also print the presentation in handout format, providing hard copy for the audience to annotate and take away for future reference.

VIEWS FOR EDITING YOUR PRESENTATION

Normal view

This is the main view and it is sub-divided into four working areas:

- **Slides tab** – lets you see each slide as a thumbnail image. You can then scroll through to see any changes you have made to the overall design. Change the order of slides by dragging them up or down; add new slides by clicking *New Slide* and selecting the desired layout; delete slides using the *Delete* key.

- **Outline tab** – lets you edit your presentation in a 'text only' environment, providing a more efficient way to draft text. Moving text between slides is easy, as is changing the order of the slides. You can also print the *Outline View* of your presentation. The *Outline* pane can be resized to see more information – simply position the mouse pointer over the right-hand edge until it changes to ✛, click and drag the pointer until it reaches the desired size. As you type, the text appears on the slide and in the *Outline View*. Using your keyboard, new lines can be created, bullets can be *promoted*/*demoted* and new slides can be inserted.

Promoting and *Demoting* changes the importance of the lines of text that you are editing:

- If you have a main point you'd like to become a sub-point, demote it!
- If you have a sub-point you'd like to become a new slide, promote it!

Example:

You want the **Sub sub title** to move down a level so that it is on a different level from the subtitle (that is, you want to decrease its importance). Select that line of text then right-click and select **Demote**. Alternatively press the **Tab** key. The **Sub sub title** has now moved to the right and the format of the bullet has changed from • to -.

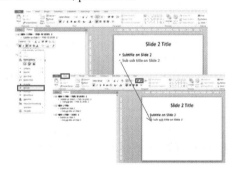

To increase the importance of text, right-click and select *Promote* or press *Shift + Tab*. The text moves left and the bullet point changes/disappears.

To create a new line at the same level, press the *Return* key.

Another way to do this is by using the *Decrease List Level* and *Increase List Level* buttons (⌐ ⌐) on the *Home* tab.

To rearrange the order of the bullets in a list right-click and select either *Move Up* or *Move Down.*

To see only the structure of the slides and not the detail, or to move slides around the *Outline* pane, right-click and select *Collapse* for one slide or *Collapse All* for every slide. To show the detail again, click on *Expand/Expand All.*

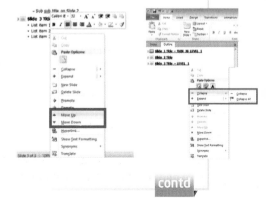

contd

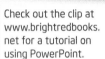

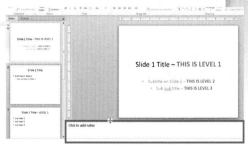

- **Slide pane** (upper-right of window) – displays a large view of the slide you are working on. From here, you can add text or any of a wide variety of graphics, video clips and animations, sounds and so on.

- **Notes pane** (below **Slide** pane) – click this pane to add notes relating to the current slide that might be useful to refer to during your presentation or reading a hard copy of it later. Notes can also be printed or posted on a Web page. The **Notes** pane can be adjusted to see all the text or it can be opened from the **View** menu. Each **Notes Page** shows a slide thumbnail, together with the notes that accompany that slide. In **Notes Page View**, you can embellish your notes with charts, pictures, tables or other illustrations and you can see how your notes pages will print. Here you can also check and change the headers and footers of your notes.

If you want to print an outline of your presentation, with the text (as it appears in **Outline View**) but no graphics or animation, you should first click the **File** tab and then click **Print**. Click **Full Page Slides** under **Settings**, then choose **Outline** from the list under **Print Layout**. Finally, click **Print** at the top.

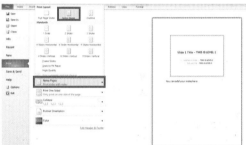

To print **Notes** – go to the **File** tab, click on **Print** then select **Notes Pages** from the drop-down menu.

The notes pages will be printed with a slide thumbnail.

To print notes pages without slide thumbnails, open each slide in **Notes Page View**, click the slide thumbnail and then press the **Delete** key before following the printing steps above.

Slide master

Slide Master View (on the **View** tab) lets you modify slides and make changes to layouts which will affect every slide in the presentation – for example insert the company logo on all slides. This saves a lot of time. **Themes** have built-in slide layouts and background graphics and you can edit these in **Slide Master View**. You can also modify individual slide layouts to change any slides using these particular layouts.

The first slide in the **Navigation** pane is the **Slide Master** and any changes made to this slide will affect the entire presentation.

Hovering the mouse over the remaining layouts will show which slides use which particular layouts. Changes to a slide layout will only be applied to those slides using that layout in your presentation.

After changing the **Slide Master**, review to see how the changes affect each slide. You may find some of your slides don't look right and more changes are needed. Click **Close Master View** to return to your presentation.

DON'T FORGET

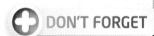

You can print only one slide thumbnail with notes per printed page.

DON'T FORGET

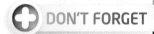

When editing an existing presentation in Slide Master view it is sometimes easier to see which layouts have been used if you first delete those layouts 'used by no slides'.

THINGS TO DO AND THINK ABOUT

It is often best to set up **Slide Master** first before creating individual slides – this can save time as you don't have to type the same information on more than one slide.

SLIDE BACKGROUNDS AND ANIMATIONS

SLIDE BACKGROUNDS

Using a picture as a slide background

You can insert a text box, WordArt or a picture behind the entire slide text as a **background** or behind part of the slide as a **watermark**, making your PowerPoint presentation unique.

Click the slide that you want to add a background picture to. On the **Design** tab click **Background Styles** and then click **Format Background**.

The **Format Background** dialog box will open. From there you can select **Fill** then **Picture or texture fill**.

To insert a picture from a file, click **File** and find the image from **Documents**. To paste a picture you have copied, click **Clipboard**. To use clip art as a background picture, click **Clip Art** and type a word or phrase describing the clip you want, or all/part of the file name in the **Search text** box.

To adjust a picture's relative lightness or transparency, slide the **Transparency** bar to the left or right, and to change the size and positioning of the graphic on the slide adjust the **Offsets** under **Stretch options**.

Finally, click **Close** to use the picture as a background for the selected slides or click **Apply to All** to use the picture on all of the slides in your presentation.

Using a colour as a slide background

Click the slide and on the **Design** tab click **Background Styles**, and then **Format Background**. When the **Format Background** dialog box opens click **Fill** and then **Solid Fill**. Select the appropriate colour and then move the **Transparency** slider.

ANIMATION BASICS FOR YOUR PRESENTATION

Animation can make a presentation dynamic and the information more memorable. The most common effects are entrances and exits. You can also add sound to increase the intensity of your animation effects.

To quickly identify if animation has been applied to a slide, look for the animation icon – a gold star which appears under the slide number in the **Slides** pane in **Normal View** and below the slide in **Slide Sorter View**.

Click on the star animation icon to preview the animation effect that has been applied to the slide.

To use entrance and exit animation effects, select the text or object in question and then, on the **Animations** tab, choose one of the many animation effects from the gallery. Clicking on the **More** arrow will give you even more options. You will see that entrance effects, emphasis effects and exit effects are green, yellow and red respectively. To change the way the text or object is animated, click

contd

Effect Options . Bear in mind, however, that not all animation effects have the same choice of ***Effect Options***.

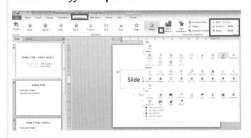

ADDING A TRANSITION TO A SLIDE

Transitions are effects that are used to add movement to your slides as you progress from one slide to another in ***Slide Show*** view. There are many transitions to choose from and each one allows you to control the speed and add sound.

Click the ***Slides*** tab and choose the thumbnail of the slide you want to apply a transition to. On the ***Transitions*** tab click the slide transition effect that you want for that slide. If you want to apply the same slide transition effect to all slides, click ***Apply To All***.

If you want to see more transition effects, click the ***More*** button .

Setting the timing for a transition

The duration of the transition between the previous slide and the current slide can be set by selecting the speed in the ***Timing*** group on the ***Transitions*** tab.

You can advance to the next slide by clicking the mouse (select the ***On Mouse Click*** check box) or you can set an amount of time before the current slide advances to the next by selecting ***After*** and then entering the number of seconds or minutes that you want.

CREATING A HYPERLINK

A **hyperlink** is a connection from one slide to another in the same presentation, to a slide in another presentation or to an e-mail address, a Web page or a file. You can create a hyperlink from text or from an object, such as a picture, graph, shape or WordArt.

In ***Normal*** view, select the text or the object that you want to use as a hyperlink and in the ***Links*** group click ***Hyperlink***.

The ***Insert Hyperlink*** box opens. Select an option in ***Link to*** then browse for a document or file, or type a web or e-mail address in the ***Address box*** and click ***OK***.

The text with the hyperlink is now underlined and will appear in blue. When viewing the presentation hover the mouse over it and the cursor will change to a hand 👆 . Click and the hyperlink will open.

THINGS TO DO AND THINK ABOUT

Head to www.brightredbooks.net to the folder called *Presentations* for a number of exercises where you can practise your skills.

Slide 3 Title – LEVEL 1

• Subtitle on Slide 3
    – Sub sub title on Slide 3

IMPORTING DATA, CHANGING MASTER HANDOUTS AND PRINTING PRESENTATIONS

ONLINE

For extra instructions on importing data from Excel into PowerPoint, head to www.brightredbooks.net

IMPORTING DATA FROM EXCEL INTO POWERPOINT

Copying a selection of cells onto a slide

Excel data can be copied and pasted into a presentation. Note, however, that the data will not update when the Excel file is changed. Select and copy the data in the Excel worksheet then click in the PowerPoint slide where you want to paste the copied worksheet data. On the *Home* tab, in the *Clipboard* group, click the arrow below *Paste*. Under *Paste Options*, do one of the following:

- Select *Keep Source Formatting* if you want to copy the data as a PowerPoint table but want it to retain the appearance of the original Excel spreadsheet.

- Select *Use Destination Styles* if you want to copy the data as a PowerPoint table but want it to assume the appearance of the PowerPoint presentation.

- Select *Embed* if you want to copy the data as information that can be edited in Excel – double-click on the data and the Excel worksheet will open.

- Select *Picture* if you want to copy the data as an uneditable picture.

- Select *Keep Text Only* if you want to copy all the data as a single text box.

Inserting a linked Excel chart

You can insert and link a chart from an Excel workbook into your PowerPoint presentation. When you edit the data in the spreadsheet, the chart on the PowerPoint slide can be easily updated.

Open the Excel workbook that has the chart that you want and select the chart. On the *Home* tab, in the *Clipboard* group, click *Copy*.

Open the PowerPoint presentation and select the slide into which you want to insert the chart.

DON'T FORGET

The workbook must be saved before the chart data can be linked in the PowerPoint file.

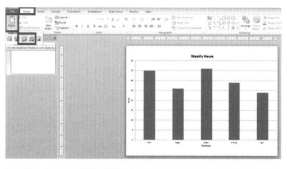

On the *Home* tab, in the *Clipboard* group, click the arrow below *Paste* and then:

- If you want the chart to look the same as it does in the Excel file, select *Keep Source Formatting & Link Data*.

- If you want the chart to assume the appearance of the PowerPoint presentation, select *Use Destination Theme & Link Data*.

When you want to update the data in the PowerPoint file, select the chart, and then under *Chart Tools*, on the *Design* tab, in the *Data* group, click *Refresh Data*.

MAKING CHANGES TO A HANDOUT MASTER

In the *Handout Master* you can make changes such as moving, resizing and formatting the header and footer placeholders. You can also set the page orientation and specify the number of slides to print per handout page.

On the *View* tab, in the *Master Views* group, click *Handout Master*. This opens the *Handout Master* tab where you can make the changes that you want. When you have finished, click *Close Master View*.

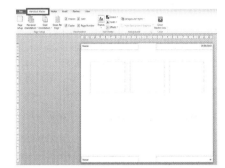

PRINTING YOUR PRESENTATION

Print is accessed from the *File* tab. There are a number of options available for printing a presentation. You may, for example, print one slide per page, three slides including lines for notes or even six or nine slides per page. These options can be accessed using the down arrow beside *Full Page Slides*.

Headers and footers can also be edited directly from this screen. Click *Edit Header & Footer* to open the *Header and Footer* dialog box where you can make changes to the *Slides* themselves and to *Notes and Handouts*.

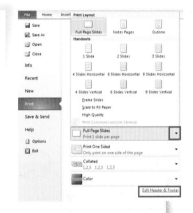

THINGS TO DO AND THINK ABOUT

Head to the digital zone to the folder called *Presentations* for a number of presentations where you can practise your skills. You will find call-outs like this throughout this book. These sample exercises are representative of SQA Higher Administration and Intermediate 2 materials 2005–15.

ELECTRONIC COMMUNICATION

E-MAIL

E-mail is a way to send and receive messages and content over the internet. It is crucial that your mailbox is managed effectively.

OUTLOOK

Outlook is a personal information manager included in the Microsoft Office suite, commonly used in the workplace. Outlook is best known as a tool for sending and receiving e-mail messages, but it also includes features for managing **calendars**, **contacts** and **tasks**. It is used in offices and workplaces to help employees communicate, manage their time and organise meetings.

GLOW

In school you will probably be using Microsoft O365 which is available through Glow and is a set of cloud-based services and tools that allow both staff and students to get access to e-mail and calendars, Office Web Apps, and video and online meetings, as well as to share documents.

 VIDEO LINK

Check out the clip at www.brightredbooks.net for more on e-mail etiquette.

 ONLINE

Follow the link at www.brightredbooks.net for more on using Outlook.

ONLINE

Not all features of e-mail and the electronic diary are currently assessed within the Administration and IT Assignment. To learn more about using the search facility, creating and managing folders, automatically managing messages and creating automated responses within Outlook head to www.brightredbooks.net.

E-MAIL ETIQUETTE

In order to ensure consistency of presentation it is important that e-mails all have the same structure. All e-mails should have:

- a subject that gives the recipient a clear idea what the message is about. Some modern business systems automatically filter out e-mails which have no subject heading.

- a proper start, for example *Dear John*. Always start a new e-mail exchange with the name of the person it is being sent to at the top.

- a sensible, relevant main message. Give the same thought and care to the composition of an e-mail as you would to a formal letter. The message should be understandable and the required actions clear. Be as concise as possible. Think about the tone, spelling and punctuation of the message as well as the content. Always be polite.

- a proper close, for example 'With regards, Tom'.

Take care with sensitive information – think about who might get to read the e-mail. A private letter may be more appropriate in some cases.

PRINTING ITEMS IN OUTLOOK

As well as printing individual e-mail messages, Contacts or Calendar items, you can also print address books, calendars or content lists of mail folders.

Whether you are in the Mail, Calendar or any other folder, click the item or folder, then click the *File* tab, then *Print*.

Under *Settings*, select a style, using *Print Preview* to help you choose from the various settings and options available. When you are ready to print, click **Print**.

THINGS TO DO AND THINK ABOUT

Head to the digital zone to the folder called *Communication* for a number of tasks where you can practise your skills.

 DON'T FORGET

For assessment purposes all printed e-mails should show evidence of sending, that is a date and time. If there is an error in the e-mail address and the e-mail 'bounces' back, then the e-mail will not have been sent and the candidate will not achieve the assessment standards for this task. In addition, all printed e-mails should be the original e-mail and not a forwarded e-mail.

 DON'T FORGET

The laws relating to written communication also apply to e-mail messages, including the Data Protection Act and the Freedom of Information Act.

 ONLINE

Not all features of the Calendar software and the Tasks software are currently assessed within the Administration and IT Assignment. To learn more about using the Task Manager, setting recurring appointments and printing selected data head to www.brightredbooks.net.

 ONLINE TEST

Test yourself on this topic at www.brightredbooks.net

DATABASES

RELATIONAL DATABASES 1

INTRODUCTION

Databases store large amounts of information in an organised and logical way. Data can be edited, updated or deleted. More importantly, finding specific information and sorting information into a particular order is very quick and easy. Data can also be imported into other applications; for example, a letter created in Word can be merged with names and addresses saved in a database.

Database software, such as Access, consists of a number of objects within a database file.

Tables

Tables contain all the information or data about a particular subject or topic; for example, the names, addresses, telephone numbers, dates of birth, subjects and exam results of all pupils in a school.

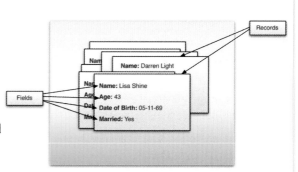

Tables are made up of **records** and each record is divided into **fields**.

A **record** is information about one person or one topic.

A **field** is a single item of information about a person or topic that appears in every record. For example, all surnames are held within the Surname field. Putting different types of information into different fields makes it easier to sort the information and to search for specific information.

Fields can be formatted for different information such as text, dates, currency, numbers and so on.

Queries

Queries are searches carried out on tables to find specific information; for example, to find all pupils with the surname Smith.

Forms

Forms are created to make it easier to input information into a table.

Reports

Reports present the information in a particular way and are produced either directly from a table or from a query.

The links between the objects in a database can be shown diagrammatically:

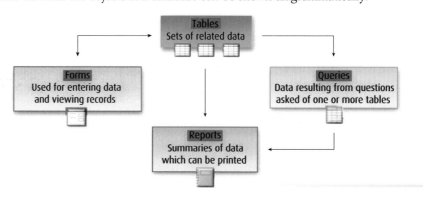

RELATIONAL DATABASES

When all the records relating to a topic or subject are held in one table, this is known as a **flat database**. However tables can become extremely large and difficult to work with and sometimes the same information might have to be keyed in repeatedly, which is not very time-efficient. Access solves this problem by allowing the user to set up a **relational database**.

A relational database has two or more tables, all of which are linked to each other. The link, or relationship, is between fields containing the same information.

Example:

There are 90 pupils in S5 and S6 who take Higher Administration and IT. Information relating to the pupils is held in one table and information relating to the teachers is held in another. In order that the information can be brought together the tables must have a relationship between them. This relationship is between the fields containing information that appears in both tables. Here, the Teacher ID field is used in both tables.

Extract from **Pupils table**
This table has a total of 90 records

Teachers table
This table has a total of 3 records. There is no need to duplicate all this information for every pupil.

These two fields contain the same information

DON'T FORGET

In some databases the field names may not be exactly the same in the different tables – it is the information within the fields that must match.

SETTING UP RELATIONSHIPS

To set up relationships you must first identify if there are any fields in any of the tables with a **primary key**. A field with a primary key contains information that will not be duplicated anywhere else in the table. In addition, the field will always contain a value – it will never be blank and it will rarely, if ever, change. The field with the primary key can, however, also be included in other tables where the data may be repeated many times. In these other tables it is called a **foreign key**. Look at this example:

Example:

In the Pupils Table the field **Pupil ID** is the field with the primary key – each pupil has a unique number which no other pupil will have. In this table it has been formatted as **AutoNumber** which means that each new pupil added to the table will automatically be allocated the next available number – if an AutoNumber is deleted it will not be reallocated.

In the Teachers table teachers all have their own unique ID number so the **Teacher ID** field will have the primary key. However **Teacher ID** also appears in the Pupils table, but because there is a Teacher ID against the name of each pupil and so the information is repeated, this means that in the Pupils table **Teacher ID** will be a foreign key.

VIDEO LINK

For more on this, watch the clip at www.brightredbooks.net

ONLINE TEST

Test yourself on relational databases at www.brightredbooks.net

 THINGS TO DO AND THINK ABOUT

Not every table has to have a primary key. Relationships can be created as long as there is one table with a primary key within any group of tables.

RELATIONAL DATABASES 2

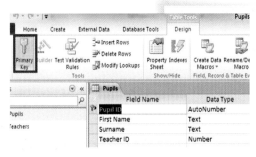

CREATING A PRIMARY KEY

To create a primary key go to **Design View** of the table and select the field that has unique information. In the **Table Tools Design** tab click on **Primary Key** .

Once all the primary keys have been created where possible, the tables can be joined using the fields that appear in more than one table – in this example it is the Teacher ID field that appears in both the Pupils table and the Teachers table.

CREATING RELATIONSHIPS

In the **Relationships** group under the **Database Tools** tab click on the **Relationships** icon.

The **Show Table** dialog box will open. Click on the table name then click on **Add**. Do this for all tables.

All tables should now appear in the **Relationships** window. Relationships are created by using the mouse and dragging the primary key field in the main table onto the field containing the same information in the associated table, that is, onto the foreign key.

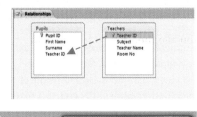

The **Edit Relationships** dialog box will open – this will show which fields from which tables are being linked. Tick the three check boxes: **Enforce Referential Integrity** (this makes sure information in one table matches information in another), **Cascade Update Related Fields** and **Cascade Delete Related Records** (these ensure any changes to one table will be reflected in other tables where relevant).

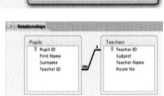

Click on **Create**.

You should now see a line joining the tables – this is the relationship.

The relationship line shows what type of relationship has been established. The example on the previous page demonstrates a 'one-to-many' relationship – 'many' being represented by the infinity symbol ∞. Here, one table contains information about pupils, the other contains a list of teachers. A one-to-many relationship has been created because one teacher can teach many pupils.

A one-to-many relationship is the most common kind of relationship. Other possible relationships are 'many-to-many', where there are many matches between the tables. For example, a pupil can take many subjects and each subject can be taken by many pupils. This type of relationship, however, requires a junction table which has fields from both tables. A 'one-to-one' relationship is also possible but is not common as most information

contd

DON'T FORGET

If there are a number of tables to be added hold down the **Shift** key on the keyboard then click on the last table name at the bottom of the list. Click on **Add** and all the tables will be added at the same time.

DON'T FORGET

Clicking and holding on the title area for each table will allow you to move the table around the **Relationships** window. You can also extend the table if necessary so you can see all the field names.

DON'T FORGET

All tables must be closed before you can create a relationship and as long as you have correctly identified all primary keys and have ensured that **Referential Integrity** has been established the computer will automatically set the relationship type. If there are any problems, they will be highlighted and you will not be able to create the relationship!

related in this manner would be in one table. A one-to-one relationship is used, for example, to divide a table with many columns or to isolate part of a table for security reasons.

Queries

Now when a *query* is created all the tables can be included in the search and the relevant fields from the appropriate tables can be selected as required.

When the query is run the results will look exactly the same as any query run on a flat database.

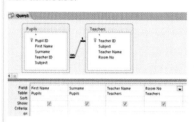 

PRINTING THE RELATIONSHIPS

You can generate a printed *Report* that shows any relationships that have been created.

In the *Tools* group under the *Relationship Tools Design* tab, click on *Relationship Report*.

A report will be generated and displayed in *Print Preview*.

Click on *Close Print Preview* and you will be taken into *Design View* where you can add your name to either of the headers or footers.

You can then return to the *Print Preview* view and click on the *Print* icon.

 ## THINGS TO DO AND THINK ABOUT

Head to www.brightredbooks.net to the folder called *Creating Relationships* where you will find a number of databases that will allow you to practise creating relationships. In each database look carefully at all the tables and identify primary keys, create the relationships and then produce a report with your name in the page footer showing the relationships that you have created.

FORMS 1

It is often easier to input data into a table using a **form**. When you create a form, you can design it to suit your purposes and so that your database makes sense to you. Forms allow you to see information already in the table and to delete or add new information. A form can also include fields from multiple tables so that you do not have to switch from one table to another to enter data.

CREATING A FORM

From the earlier example, you might want to see a teacher's record from one table and information about that teacher's pupils from another table at the same time.

Using the **Form Wizard**, which can be found in the **Forms** group on the **Create** tab, is the most straightforward method of creating a form exactly as you want as the wizard guides you through a number of steps.

When working with a relational database you often need to view data from more than one table on the same form. In these cases you will want to create a **subform**.

A subform is a form that is inserted into the main form. These are especially effective when you want to show data from tables or queries that have a one-to-many relationship: that is, where one record in the primary table corresponds to many records in the related table. For example, you can create a form that displays the teacher's data and contains a subform that displays each pupil. The data in the Teachers Table is the 'one' side of the relationship. The data in the Pupils Table is the 'many' side of the relationship (since each teacher can have more than one pupil).

The main form and subform are linked so that the subform displays only records that are related to the current record in the main form. For example, when the main form displays Mrs Parker's information, the subform displays only her pupils. If the form and subform were unlinked, the subform would display all the pupils, not just Mrs Parker's.

The **Form Wizard** will allow you to create a form with or without a subform.

The main form shows data from the 'one' side of the relationship.

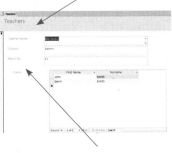

The subform shows data from the 'many' side of the relationship.

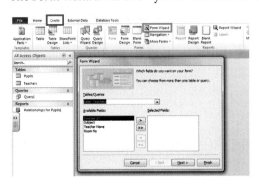

Clicking on **Form Wizard** under the **Create** tab will open the **Form Wizard** dialog box where you can select a table or query from the **Tables/Queries** drop-down list. Double-click on the fields that you want to include from the table or query. Continue to select another table or query from the list and double-click on the fields that you want. When you have completed your selection, click on **Next**.

VIEWING YOUR DATA

Assuming you set up a one-to-many relationship, the second window of the wizard will now ask you *How do you want to view your data?* and will give you two options.

Choice 1 – set up the form with one or more subforms

Select *by Teachers*. Fields from the Teachers Table will make up the main form while fields from the Pupils Table will make up the subform. This form will show one teacher and all the pupils relating to that teacher.

Choice 2 – set up a single form

Select *by Pupils*. This form will show all the information relating to one pupil.

Click *Next* when you have made your choice.

The third window will let you choose the layout of your form – the choices will vary depending whether you have chosen to have a subform or not.

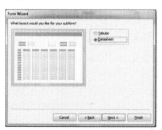

Form with subform – both these layout styles arrange the subform data in rows and columns. You can customise the **Tabular** layout, whereas **Datasheet** is more compact and looks like the datasheet view of a table.

Single form – there are four choices of layout. **Columnar** is probably most user-friendly and is easy to customise.

Form with subform – both forms can have different titles.

The fourth window will allow you to key in titles for your form and subform. Again, the window will vary slightly depending on whether you have a subform or a single form.

Once you have keyed in the title(s), you now have the same choice for both types of form. You can either open the form or subform so that you can view or enter information *or* you can open in *Design View* so that you can modify the design of the form. Once you have made your choice click on *Finish* and your form will be created.

Single form – give your form an appropriate title.

Single form

Form including subform

 ## THINGS TO DO AND THINK ABOUT

- If you choose to have a subform Access will automatically save both the main form including the subform and the subform only. Make sure you open the main form when you want to use it to update your database.

- To add a new record to all forms/subforms click on the *New* (blank) record button.
- To delete a record go to the *Home* tab and *Records* and using the drop-down menu beside *Delete* click on .

Once you delete the record you cannot undo your deletion so always ensure you are deleting the correct one!

ONLINE

Try out the extension tasks at www.brightredbooks.net to practise your skills.

ONLINE TEST

Head to www.brightredbooks.net and test yourself on forms.

FORMS 2

DON'T FORGET

Can't see any of the tables, queries, forms or reports you have created? Ensure you select **All Access Objects** in the **Navigation** pane on the left-hand side of your screen.

ONLINE

Try out the extension tasks at www.brightredbooks.net to practise your skills.

DON'T FORGET

To edit a label and put the text onto two or more lines, hold down the **Shift** key and press the **Return** key at the same time.

DON'T FORGET

In **Design View** make sure you know the difference between the boxes containing **labels** and the boxes containing the information that comes directly from the database fields. If you make changes to the wrong box you may end up with an error. If you make a mistake in the form just start again and work through the wizard – it will be quicker in the long run!

EDITING THE LAYOUT OF A FORM

Small changes to forms can be made in **Layout View** which means that you can actually see how the form will look while you are moving things around.

An orange border will appear around any field you click on. When your cursor changes into a double-headed black arrow ⟷ you can change the size, whilst a four-headed arrow ✛ indicates that you can move the field.

You can also edit labels but note that any changes will not change the field headings in the table. Only changes to records will be reflected in the tables.

To make more complex changes to the form/subform click on **View** and switch to **Design View**.

The **Form Design Tools** will become available to you.

Expand the list of tools available under the **Design** tab. The **label** tool and the **image** tool are the two that you will use most.

The **label** tool will let you draw text boxes, for example when you want to insert your name in the footer.

The **image** tool will let you insert a picture or graphic that has been saved in your **My Pictures** folder.

Click on the **image** tool and move into the area where you would like the graphic to appear (normally the **Form Header**). Draw a square and your **Documents** folder will open, allowing you to search for your saved image. If your image is cut off when it is inserted click on the **Property Sheet** icon in the **Design** tab. In the **Property Sheet** ensure **Size Mode** is set to **Zoom**.

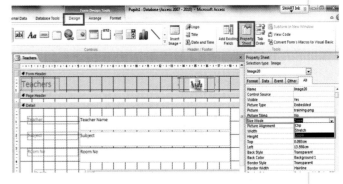

To move the subform independently of its label click on the grey handle (rectangle) at the top left of the subform and your cursor will change to a four-headed arrow (✛), allowing you to move the subform.

contd

To line up labels and objects in your form click the first label and hold down the **Shift** key on your keyboard then click on any other label or object so that everything you want lined up is highlighted. Go to the **Align** button in the **Sizing and Ordering** group of the **Arrange** tab under **Form Design Tools**. Selecting **Left** will move all the highlighted objects to align with the one that is sitting furthest left. You can do the same to align to the right, top or bottom.

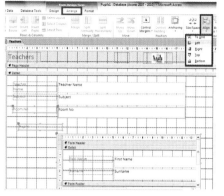

The **Size/Space** tools are also useful and will save you time when you are trying to make the form look neat. For example, you can select all the boxes and make them all the same height as the shortest.

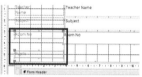

In **Design View** the **Form Header** and **Form Footer** are automatically shown. Right-click with your mouse in the **Form Header** area to show **Page Header/Footer**.

PRINTING A FORM

To print only one record in **Form View**, display that record on your screen. Go to **File** then **Print** and in the **Print** dialog box click on **Selected Record(s)** then click **OK**.

THINGS TO DO AND THINK ABOUT

Head to the digital zone to the folder called *Creating Forms* for a number of databases where you can practise creating forms.

QUERIES

A **query** lets you search for specific information in a table. The results of the query can be sorted and printed in the same way as when you are dealing with tables. Queries can be saved for future use and can be edited later. Queries are also dynamic, which means that if data in the table changes the query based on that table will automatically be updated when the table is opened again.

CREATING A QUERY

First, in the **Create** tab select **Query Design**.

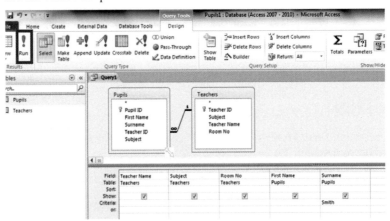

The **Show Table** dialog box will open.
Select the table or tables you want to run your search on and click on **Add**.

All the selected tables can now be seen in the **Query design** pane and you will be able to see the relationships that have been set.

Double-click each field name from the appropriate table that you want included in your search. The grid will show both the fields you have chosen and which table they have been taken from.

Use the **Criteria** line to key in the information you want to search for then click on the **Run** icon ! on the ribbon.

QUERIES AT HIGHER LEVEL

At Higher level, queries are more complex than at N4 and N5, and usually involve up to four criteria. Most searches you have carried out until now have involved finding an exact match of a word or words you are looking for under the appropriate field, or finding dates or numbers using mathematical symbols such as > for 'greater than'. The following table is a summary of the different parameters you will now be expected to use.

CRITERIA	WHAT TO KEY IN	EXAMPLE	WHAT THE QUERY WILL FIND
To find an exact match of a word	Key in the word	= "Glasgow" Note: the computer will automatically assume you mean equal to and will insert = and " " around the word	Glasgow
To find both words	word **and** word	"Smith" and "Jones"	Smith <u>and</u> Jones
To find either or	word **or** word	"Glasgow" or "Edinburgh"	Glasgow <u>or</u> Edinburgh
To exclude records	**Not** word	Not "Glasgow"	All towns except Glasgow
To search for empty fields	Is null	Is null	Any records where there is an empty field
To search for fields that contain text or a value	Is not null	Is not null	Records within the table that do not have any empty fields
To find a word in a list or a word that contains these letters – the * represents any other letters or words	*	Th* *Admin*	the, them, they, there, that, and so on Admin, Administration, Office Administration, Admin and IT, and so on
To find a *single* alphabetic character	?	Sm?th	Smith, Smyth but not smooth
To find a *single* numeric character	#	5#6	506, 516, 526, and so on
Numbers and currency Greater than Greater than or equal to Less than Less than or equal to Between	 > >= < <= Between value and value	 >12 >=10 <8 <=4 Between 45 and 50	 Any number higher than 12 10 and anything above it Any number lower than 8 4 and anything below it Numbers between 45 and 50, including 45 and 50
Dates Before After Between dates	 < > between (date) and (date)	 <1 5 16 >30 4 15 Between 1 1 15 and 31 12 15	 Dates before 1 May 2016 Dates after 30 April 2015 Dates between 1 January and 31 December 2015 including 1 January and 31 December
Yes/No ✓	Yes	Yes	All Yes records

NOTES: Do not include the £ sign when looking for currency amounts.

Do not include commas in any figures.

You will need to insert " " around any phrases that use the word 'and', for example "Highlands and Islands".

Because date fields are formatted as dates you can key in the day, month and year as numbers and with a space between each – the result will be shown in the format chosen, for example long date or short date.

Field:	ID	Surname	First	Date of Birth	Address	Town	Postcode	Cou
Table:	Pupils	Pupils	Pupils	Pupils	Pupils	Pupils	Pupils	Pup
Sort:								
Show:	☑	☑	☑	☑	☑	☑	☑	
Criteria:				Between #01/01/2002# And #31/12/2002#				
or:								

THINGS TO DO AND THINK ABOUT

Head to the digital zone to the folder called *Queries* for a number of databases where you can practise creating queries.

DON'T FORGET

Your queries will be made up of a variety of these parameters – not just one!

DON'T FORGET

Run your query each time you add criteria to check that you have entered it correctly. If you enter a lot of criteria and get no results it may be difficult to spot where the error lies.

DON'T FORGET

When you key in your criteria, let the computer add any relevant syntax, for example dates make use of #.

DON'T FORGET

Always key in all the search criteria in the single line that says *Criteria*. Never use the line that says *or* – this could lead to problems!

VIDEO LINK

Learn more about this by watching the clip at www.brightredbooks.net

ONLINE TEST

Test yourself on queries at www.brightredbooks.net

CALCULATED AND AGGREGATE QUERIES

CALCULATED QUERIES

Create a new field to perform a **calculation** using numerical values from existing fields by setting up a query which includes the calculation. This ensures that any changes made to information in the table are used when the query is run.

For example, pupils' marks for their Administration exam (two papers) have been added to the database. To find the total mark achieved by pupils taught by Mrs Hill (Teacher ID 2) without seeing this field, run a query as shown on the right in *Design View*.

The results will look like this:

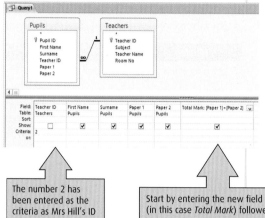

First Name	Surname	Paper 1	Paper 2	Total Mark
Gill	Gordon	32	29	61
Jordan	Grant	29	29	58
Jason	Stevenson	37	36	73
Kirsty	Jacobs	41	34	75
Malcom	Allan	28	34	62

Once you have a new field you can use this name in a further calculation. Doing extra homework might help increase the total mark by 10%. To find 10% of their total mark, run a query as shown on the right.

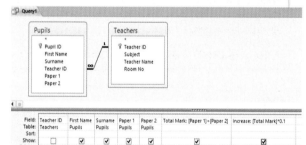

The results now look like this:

First Name	Surname	Paper 1	Paper 2	Total Mark	Increase
Gill	Gordon	32	29	61	6.1
Jordan	Grant	29	29	58	5.8
Jason	Stevenson	37	36	73	7.3
Kirsty	Jacobs	41	34	75	7.5
Malcom	Allan	28	34	62	6.2

To change the format of the calculation, go to *Design View* and either right-click and select *Properties...* or click on *Property Sheet* in the *Design* ribbon. Choose *Fixed* for numbers or *Currency* for money.

DON'T FORGET

The mathematical symbols are the same as those used in a spreadsheet:
+ for addition
– for subtraction
* for multiplication
/ for division

DON'T FORGET

The text in the grid is quite small and can be difficult to read. To make it easier to see what you have keyed in go to *Design View*, click on the text and hold down the *Shift* key and the *F2* key at the same time. The *Zoom* window will open, allowing you to select a larger font size to view the calculation.

DON'T FORGET

Ensure you maintain the same format for the new field name label as for the existing field names. For example, are existing field names all in capital letters or with initial capitals only?

DON'T FORGET

If the results of your calculation show ###### it is because the field is too narrow – simply double-click on the line to the right of the column to widen it. Remember too to open *Property Sheet* and select the appropriate format, for example *Fixed* if it is a number and the number of decimal places.

The number 2 has been entered as the criteria as Mrs Hill's ID is 2 and the tick has been removed from the *Show* box as you do not want to see this field when the query is run

Start by entering the new field name (in this case *Total Mark*) followed by :
then key in each existing field name enclosed by square brackets and the appropriate mathematical symbol (in this example the calculation is an addition so + has been used)

IT IS EXTREMELY IMPORTANT THAT YOU FOLLOW THESE CONVENTIONS OF USING THE COLON AND SQUARE BRACKETS SO THAT ACCESS KNOWS WHEN A FIELD STARTS AND ENDS AND WHEN THE CALCULATION BEGINS

The new field name is Increase and the previous new field name Total Mark is now treated as if it was an existing field name so it is enclosed in square brackets.

IT IS VERY IMPORTANT TO NOTE THAT YOU CANNOT USE THE % SYMBOL IN YOUR CALCULATION – YOU MUST CONVERT THE PERCENTAGE FIGURE TO A DECIMAL NUMBER eg 10% is 0.10, 2% is 0.02 etc

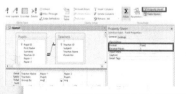

Teacher Name	AvgOfPaper	AvgOfPaper
Mr Bonas	37	############
Mrs Hill	33.4	32.4
Mrs Parker	39.5	32

Teacher Name	AvgOfPaper 1	AvgOfPaper 2
Mr Bonas	37.0	34.7
Mrs Hill	33.4	32.4
Mrs Parker	39.5	32.0

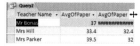

contd

Calculation including a percentage increase

You now want to calculate the total mark including a 10% increase.

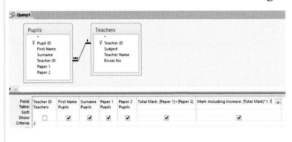

This is the same as calculating Total Mark + (10% * Total Mark). Do this quickly by taking the original mark and multiplying by 1·10. The query looks like this:

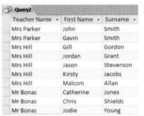

You can use this method to add any percentage to an original number.

AGGREGATE QUERIES

Aggregate queries (or **totals queries**) allow data to be grouped so a calculation can be performed on the grouping.

In this database there are three teachers. To find how many pupils there are in each teacher's class, include both the names of the teachers and the pupils in the query.

When the query is run the data is not grouped and each teacher's name is repeated. Running a **totals query** will group all the teachers' names, and using the **Count** function will find out how many pupils each teacher has.

To construct a totals query: go to **Design View** and click on the **Totals** button Σ in the **Show/Hide** group on the **Design** ribbon under **Query Tools**.

A **Total** row will be added below **Table** in the design grid. All values in that row are set by default to **Group By**. Go to the field and select the calculation. In this example you want to count the number of pupils in each class so select **Count**.

Hint: the first field in the design grid should remain **Group By**. Read your instructions carefully and look out for the phrase 'for each...' – this is normally the field that you would **Group By**. When you run the query for this example, the results will look like this:

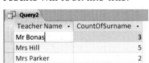

The field is automatically renamed according to the calculation. Note that there are no spaces between the words in this new field name.

The field name can be amended in **Design View**. Click immediately before it (it still appears as Surname) and key the new name followed by a colon (:). Now run the query again. Note that the colon is extremely important. It comes immediately after the new field name and before the existing one.

Other examples of calculations used in a totals query are:

Sum totals numbers for the group

Avg finds the group average

Min finds the lowest number in the group

Max finds the highest number in the group.

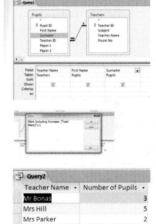

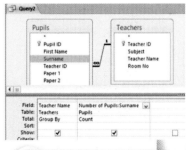

VIDEO LINK

Check out the clips at www. brightredbooks.net to learn more on this topic.

 THINGS TO DO AND THINK ABOUT

Head to the digital zone to the folders called *Calculations in Queries* and *Aggregate Queries* for a number of exercises where you can practise setting up these types of queries.

REPORTS 1

A **database report** allows you to summarise and print information from a database table or query. Once a report has been created it can be run at any time and will always reflect the current data from the database – additions, deletions or amendments to the table will also be reflected in the report. Reports are normally formatted to be printed but they can also be viewed on screen, exported to another programme or sent as part of an e-mail.

REPORT WIZARD

Using the **Report Wizard** is the most straightforward method of creating a report and is very similar to using the **Form Wizard**. The **Report Wizard** can be found in the **Reports** group under the **Create** tab.

The **Report Wizard** provides a number of steps which will enable you to select the source for your report – multiple tables and/or queries – as well as the fields you want to include and how you want the information organised.

At Higher level you will be presented with quite a lot of information and instructions in the form of a paragraph and you have to decide what criteria to use in the search on which the report will be based. Take a highlighter pen and highlight all the key instructions.

Example:

Find pupils who attained 30 or more for both Paper 1 and Paper 2. Present this information grouped by teacher in the form of a report. (*Hint: Create a query then run it to ensure no errors.*)
In the report sort students by Surname but ensure that First Name appears before Surname. Include an appropriate graphic (something to do with computers) in the report header.

STEPS TO BE FOLLOWED WHEN CREATING A REPORT

Step 1

Create a query with the fields to be searched using the given criteria. Also include all the other fields that will appear in the report.

Run the query to make sure you have all the information you need.

Do not group any of the information in this query – it is NOT an aggregate query. The grouping instruction in this task is a layout instruction, not a calculation instruction so do not click on . In this task, grouping will be done in the **Report Wizard**.

Teacher Name	First Name	Surname	Paper 1	Paper 2
Mrs Parker	Gavin	Smith	36	32
Mrs Parker	John	Smith	43	32
Mrs Hill	Kirsty	Jacobs	41	34
Mr Bonas	Chris	Shields	40	36
Mrs Hill	Jason	Stevenson	37	36
Mr Bonas	Catherine	Jones	45	42

Save the query in case you want to use it again or make changes.

Step 2

Open the **Report Wizard**, find the query you have saved and use 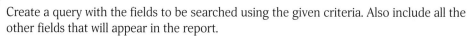 to take all the fields to be included in the report into the **Selected Fields** window. Click **Next**.

At this stage it is a good idea to try to visualise how you would like your report to look so that you can select the fields in the order that you want them to appear in the report – this can save time if you have to edit the layout later, especially if you are working with a large number of fields.

contd

Step 3

The second window asks **How do you want to view your data?** This is where you must look carefully for any grouping instructions.

This example asked you to group by teacher so ensure that **by Teachers** is selected. By doing this each teacher's name will be the first column in the report. Grouping also automatically sorts the field alphabetically. Each teacher's name will only appear once in the first column of the report with all relevant students listed to the right of the teacher's name. Click on **Next**.

Step 4

The third window will give you the opportunity to add any further groupings. There are no other groupings in this example so click **Next**.

(This window does not always appear – it will depend upon the information included in your query.)

Step 5

This window gives you the opportunity to sort your data. However the fields you choose to sort by will then move to become the next column(s) in your report after the field you grouped by. For example, if you choose to sort by Surname at this point it will appear in your report before First Name. You may not want this layout in the final report. So as not to waste time rearranging columns in **Design View** there is an option to **Group & Sort** in **Design View** once your report has been completed (this method is shown on page 31). As this example instructs that First Name appears before Surname do not select any sorting here – simply click on **Next**.

Step 6

You must now decide how you would like your report laid out. Layout is normally **Stepped**. However think carefully if you want **Portrait** or **Landscape Orientation**. If a lot of fields have been included in the report or the information in any field is particularly long and detailed, then select **Landscape**. Note that it is far easier to choose the orientation at this point rather than change it when your report is complete.

Step 7

The final step is to choose a relevant title for your report. The title should reflect the query/instructions.

Click on **Finish**.

Your report will now be generated and will appear on your screen in **Print Preview**.

THINGS TO DO AND THINK ABOUT

Most of the text that you see in any of the headers or footers is actually a label. Labels can be edited as you would in a Word document – the exception is in the page footer where the date and page numbering are inserted automatically and so the information is based on coded text. Either leave these as they are or delete – do not attempt to edit these.

Similarly, the information coming from the fields of the database table is displayed in the **Detail** area of the form and should not be edited or deleted.

VIDEO LINK

Watch the video at www.brightredbooks.net to learn more about queries.

ONLINE TEST

Head to www.brightredbooks.net and test yourself on reports.

REPORTS 2

FINAL STEP – TIDYING UP YOUR REPORT

You haven't finished your report yet! There is information that has been 'truncated' (cut off), and you still have to sort pupils into alphabetical order by Surname.

Click on **Close Print Preview** and you will be taken into **Design View**.

There are five main sections in a basic report:

1 **Report Header** – appears once on the first page.
2 **Page Header** – appears at the top of every page of the report. It contains the field names as they appear in the table or query. These appear as column headings in the report.
3 **Detail** – contains the data; that is, the records which are to be displayed in the report.
4 **Page Footer** – appears at the bottom of every page and contains today's date and the page number by default.
5 **Report Footer** – appears on the last page of the report before the page footer. It can contain items such as column totals.

Labels and fields can now be moved around the page to give you the layout you want or to improve the presentation of the data. For example, you can reduce the size of the labels and the fields for Teacher Name, First Name and Surname and this will give you room to move and resize Paper 1 and Paper 2 labels and fields so that all the information is visible.

EDITING YOUR REPORT

- Always ensure you work within the space you are given – do not extend the area of the report at the right-hand side otherwise you will be creating new pages with information split at inappropriate points. Try to select the correct page orientation in the wizard rather than changing it after the report has been generated.
- If you have to rearrange or resize a lot of fields stop what you are doing and start again – the wizard is quick to work through and you may be able to make some changes at various steps which will improve the layout. You will save yourself time in the long run!
- Select more than one field and/or label at the same time by clicking on one field/label box then holding down the **Shift** key on the keyboard and selecting other boxes. They can now all be moved as a group at the same time.
- Make use of the **Align** button which is available in the **Sizing and Ordering** group which is on the **Arrange** tab under **Report Design Tools** to line up the boxes accurately. This is similar to working in the **Design View** of a **form**.
- If you are really struggling for space you can highlight all the labels or all the fields and select a smaller font size. This might be enough to save you moving labels/fields to create space.
- As soon as you have made any changes to the layout of your report switch to **Print Preview** – if there are any problems you can go back to **Design View** and use the undo button.

ONLINE TEST

Head to
www.brightredbooks.net
and test yourself on reports.

contd

- If there is a field in the database that contains a lot of information, do not adjust the size of the box. Instead, click on **Property Sheet** and under the **All** tab go to **Can Grow** and **Can Shrink** and select **Yes** for both. The computer will now allow the box to expand horizontally to accommodate all the information.

Sorting in design view

To sort after the report has been generated click on the **Group & Sort** button in the **Grouping & Totals** group of the **Design** tab under **Report Design Tools**.

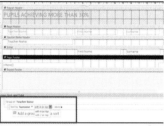

Click on **Add a Sort** and choose the relevant field from the list that is displayed, then click on the order of the sort. To remove the sort click on ✕

Note that any grouping levels will also be shown here. In this example **Group by Teacher Name** was selected in the second window of the wizard.

Adding a graphic to the report

To add a graphic to the **Page Header** click on the **Image** button in the **Design** palette as you would in a form and draw a square where you want the image to appear. Your **Documents** folder will open and you can search for your saved image.

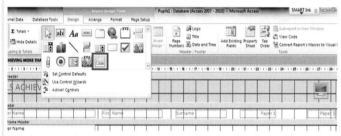

To ensure that the picture is displayed in full and can be resized easily, select **Size Mode Zoom** under the **All** tab in the **Property Sheet**.

The final report will look something like this:

THINGS TO DO AND THINK ABOUT

Head to the digital zone to the folders called *Reports* and *Calculated Reports* for a number of exercises where you can practise running queries and creating reports.

REPORTS 3

CALCULATIONS IN A REPORT

It is possible to carry out **summaries of numeric values** within a report, but only if the information is grouped in some way. For example, you might want to summarise pupils' marks by teacher and find the average mark for Paper 1 and Paper 2.

Start the report as you normally would – either select the appropriate fields directly from each table or create a *Query*. Click on *Next*.

In the second window of the wizard you must ensure you have grouped the data – here it is grouped by Teachers.

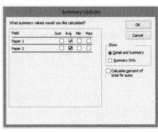

In the next window you will see the ***Summary Options...*** button. This button will not appear if the information has not been grouped in the previous window.

Click on the ***Summary Options...*** button and the **Summary Options** window will open. Here you will see all the fields that have a numeric value.

You can choose what type of calculation you want to carry out:

Sum will add the numbers in the grouping.

Avg will find the group average.

Min will find the lowest number in the group.

Max will find the highest number in the group.

You can *Show* either:

- ***Detail and Summary*** – you will see all the information that makes up the grouping – in this case all the pupils' names as well as the average marks.

or

- ***Summary Only*** – you will not see pupils' names; you will only see the average mark for the grouping.

Click *OK* when you have made your choice. The remaining steps of the wizard are the same as for a basic report.

DON'T FORGET

For most reports that you are asked to produce you will show the *Detail and Summary*.

When all steps of the wizard have been completed the report that is generated will look similar to this:

PUPILS' AVERAGE MARKS

Teacher Name	First Name	Surname	Paper 1	Paper 2
Mrs Parker				
	Gavin	Smith	38	32
	John	Smith	43	32
Summary for 'Teacher ID' = 1 (2 detail records)				
Avg			39.5	32
Mrs Hill				
	Malcom	Allan	28	34
	Kirsty	Jacobs	41	34
	Jason	Stevenson	37	36
	Jordan	Grant	29	29
	Gill	Gordon	32	29
Summary for 'Teacher ID' = 2 (5 detail records)				
Avg			33.4	32.4
Mr Bonas				
	Jodie	Young	26	26
	Chris	Shields	40	36
	Catherine	Jones	45	42
Summary for 'Teacher ID' = 3 (3 detail records)				
Avg			37	34.66667

Note that just as in the previous report Teachers are grouped but the *Report Wizard* has now calculated the average mark for each teacher's pupils.

Above the average, an additional summary line has been automatically included. It is not needed and can be deleted in *Design View*.

In *Design View* you will see that a new

contd

footer has been created which shows the calculation. Delete the **Summary for** line and edit the label to become more meaningful. For example, Avg can be amended to Class Average.

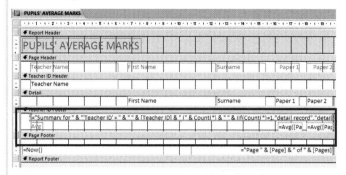

Additional editing of this report would include ensuring all information is visible and there is no truncated text and that numbers are formatted appropriately – for example, in this case the averages are formatted to whole numbers. To do this, open the **Property Sheet** and under the **All** tab change the **Format** of the number field to **Fixed** and select the required number of decimal places – in this case 0.

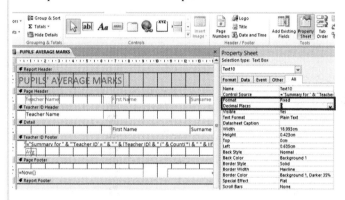

Return to **Print Preview** and the finished report now looks far more professional and presentable.

 THINGS TO DO AND THINK ABOUT

Head to the digital zone to the folders called *Reports* and *Calculated Reports* for a number of exercises where you can practise running queries and creating reports.

 **DON'T FORGET**

Choosing **Sum** within the **Summary Options** window will produce an overall grand total as well as a total for each group. The grand total will appear in the report footer.

 **DON'T FORGET**

Subtotals or totals not displaying in your report? If you have used grouping within a query unnecessarily – that is, you have used the ∑ button and mistakenly created an aggregate query – the **Enter Parameter Value** window may appear on your screen. Unless you enter a relevant value this field in your report will remain blank. Check the query again to ensure it is correct.

 VIDEO LINK

Learn more about reports by watching the clip at www.brightredbooks.net

 ONLINE TEST

Head to www.brightredbooks.net and test yourself on reports.

INTEGRATION OF DATABASES

USING A DATABASE TO CREATE MAILING LABELS

Access has a label wizard that can be used to create and print a report that is formatted to fit **mailing labels**. Information such as names and addresses can be taken either directly from a table or from the results of running a query. Mailing labels are a quick and efficient way of preparing envelopes for posting.

Open the table or query you want to use as the source of data for your labels. Imagine, for example, that you want to send pupils a letter via their teacher. A query has been set up showing pupils' names, teachers' names and the room number of the class.

In the *Reports* group under the *Create* tab click on *Labels* and the *Label Wizard* will open.

ONLINE

Learn about sorting on two or more fields within a table or query at www.brightredbooks.net

The first step is to select the labels that will be used. Most stationery manufacturers are listed along with the product codes of the various label sizes they produce. It is very unlikely that you will use actual sheets of labels in the classroom – rather you will print on plain paper. Your layout, however, should still reflect how a sheet of labels would actually look. So choose, for example, Avery L7160 (which has three labels across and seven labels down on size A4 paper).

Click on *Next*.

The font name, size, weight and text colour wanted for the label can be chosen in the second window. Unless there are any specific instructions accept the defaults and click on *Next*.

The third window allows you to select the fields needed and the layout of the label. Double-click each field you want to add or select the field and click on ▶. Remember to add spaces between fields or returns when you want a new line and so on. Click on *Next*.

The second-last window gives the option of sorting the labels, for example by surname. Click on *Next*.

The final window lets you give your report a name – this will not appear on the labels but it is useful if you want to re-run the report and print the same labels again at a later date.

Your completed labels will look similar to this:

It is possible to go to *Design View* to add your name to the page footer. There should be as few further edits to labels as possible. If there are a lot of changes to be made to the layout of the label simply work through the *Label Wizard* again.

Label Design View

EXPORTING FROM ACCESS TO OTHER APPLICATIONS

One of the benefits of working with applications from the same software package is that the programs work well together and information from one application can be used in another. Two ways to do this are:

Copying and pasting

Tables and queries can be selected then copied and pasted into another application, for example Word or PowerPoint, and can then be edited using the usual edit menu choices.

Linking objects

When an object is linked, the information in the file you have copied it to (the destination) is updated if the source file is modified.

COPYING FROM A TABLE OR QUERY INTO AN EXISTING WORD DOCUMENT OR POWERPOINT PRESENTATION

Data from a table or a query can be copied and pasted into an existing Word document by clicking at the top left-hand corner of the table or query so that the entire table/query is selected and then clicking on **Copy** from the **Home** ribbon and then clicking **Paste** in the Word document. A table has now been created in Word which can be edited and formatted using the usual **Table Tools** commands.

You can use the same method to copy and paste from Access into a PowerPoint presentation.

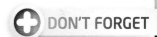

DON'T FORGET

When a table is copied into Word or PowerPoint the name of the database table automatically becomes the first row in the table. This row can be deleted using **Table Tools**.

EXPORTING FROM A TABLE, QUERY OR REPORT INTO A NEW WORD DOCUMENT

Using the **Export Wizard** allows a database file to be exported into a new Word document. Data from a table, a query or a report can be copied into a Word Rich Text Format file (*.rtf). Both the data and its layout are copied to closely resemble the original report format.

Under the **External Data** tab select **More** from the **Export** group then click on **Word** from the drop-down menu.

Browse to ensure the file will be saved in the correct location and tick the box marked **Open the destination file after export operation is complete** and click **OK**.

The table is now published in a text file and can be edited and formatted using Word commands. For example, you can choose to **AutoFit to Window** if the table is too large for the page.

ONLINE

Learn about linking a database object in a word document at www.brightredbooks.net

ONLINE TEST

Head to www.brightredbooks.net and test yourself on databases.

 THINGS TO DO AND THINK ABOUT

Head to the digital zone to the folder called *Integration of Databases* for a number of exercises where you can practise integrating data from a database with other applications.

WORD PROCESSING

BUSINESS DOCUMENTS: LETTERS AND ITINERARIES

There are a number of documents that businesses use on a daily basis to communicate with both staff and customers. Organisations often follow their own house style or make use of **document templates** (stored centrally and available to all employees) to save time and ensure consistency of presentation.

DON'T FORGET

Business letters sometimes go over two or more pages. Always number all pages either in the header or the footer, except for the first page.

BUSINESS LETTERS

A **business letter** is a document written in formal language and sent to customers, suppliers or other organisations.

Example:

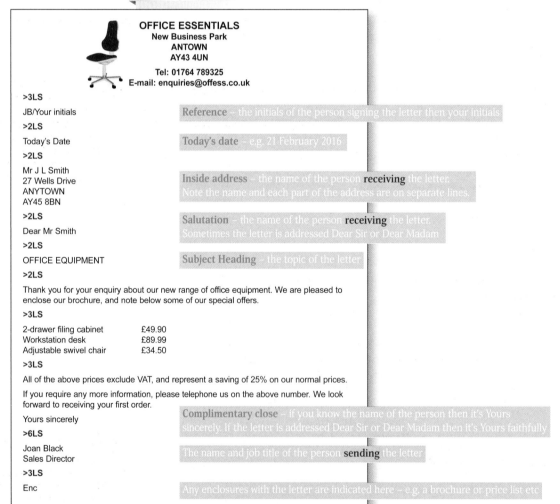

OFFICE ESSENTIALS
New Business Park
ANTOWN
AY43 4UN

Tel: 01764 789325
E-mail: enquiries@offess.co.uk

>3LS

JB/Your initials — **Reference** – the initials of the person signing the letter then your initials

>2LS

Today's Date — **Today's date** – e.g. 21 February 2016

>2LS

Mr J L Smith
27 Wells Drive
ANYTOWN
AY45 8BN — **Inside address** – the name of the person **receiving** the letter. Note the name and each part of the address are on separate lines.

>2LS

Dear Mr Smith — **Salutation** – the name of the person **receiving** the letter. Sometimes the letter is addressed Dear Sir or Dear Madam

>2LS

OFFICE EQUIPMENT — **Subject Heading** – the topic of the letter

>2LS

Thank you for your enquiry about our new range of office equipment. We are pleased to enclose our brochure, and note below some of our special offers.

>3LS

2-drawer filing cabinet £49.90
Workstation desk £89.99
Adjustable swivel chair £34.50

>3LS

All of the above prices exclude VAT, and represent a saving of 25% on our normal prices.

If you require any more information, please telephone us on the above number. We look forward to receiving your first order.

Yours sincerely — **Complimentary close** – if you know the name of the person then it's Yours sincerely. If the letter is addressed Dear Sir or Dear Madam then it's Yours faithfully

>6LS

Joan Black
Sales Director — The name and job title of the person **sending** the letter

>3LS

Enc — Any enclosures with the letter are indicated here – e.g. a brochure or price list etc

Tear-off slips

A letter occasionally has a **tear-off slip** for the recipient to give a response. Always place the tear-off portion near the bottom of the page and use double line spacing to ensure there is enough room for any written information.

contd

Tear-off slips can be created by setting tabs as required with the tab at the right margin being a **right tab**. Dots or a solid line can then be chosen from **Leader** options.

The scissors can be found in the **Symbol** window – select the font **Wingdings**.

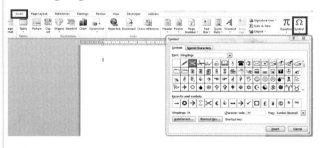

Quadrant International
Design Specialists
14 Union Square
ABERDEEN
AB4 8ET

Tel: 01224 351221   E-mail: Quad@dmail.com

JL/JS

8 March 2016

Candlelight Design
291 Sauchie Street
GLASGOW
G12 2LH

Dear Sirs

NEW PRODUCTIONS

We have just received advance samples of 8 designs by Mario and Fabia Manzini. The new designs are lively and attractive and are exactly what we have come to expect from these very talented artists. The designs will be reproduced in fabrics suitable for window dressing and upholstery as well as wall coverings.

Mario and Fabia have extended their range and have included matching accessories – throws, cushions and rugs. This colour and theme co-ordinated range is most attractive and makes room decoration a positive art! If you would like to see the new range simply complete the attached tear-off slip and return it to us in the enclosed reply-paid envelope and we will send you samples by return.

Yours faithfully

J Lennon
Publicity Manager

Enc

 ....

I am very interested in the new designs/accessories by Mario and Fabia Manzini.

Signed .... Date ....

Position in Company ....

Address ....

.... Postcode ....

* Delete as appropriate

ITINERARIES

An **itinerary** is a detailed plan for a journey listing hour by hour what a person is scheduled to do, as well as where and with whom they are scheduled to do it. All times are expressed in 24-hour format and, where there are time differences, local times are shown.

ITINERARY: Peter Black   Make use of bold to highlight headings
>2LS
Final of 'Young Project Manager of the Year', Liverpool
>2LS
Saturday 15 February – Sunday 16 February 2014
>3LS
Saturday 15 February
>2 LS

1123 hours	Train departs Pitlochry station to Edinburgh Waverley station
1323 hours	Arrive Edinburgh Waverley station
1416 hours	Depart Edinburgh Waverley station to Preston station
1648 hours	Arrive Preston station
1704 hours	Depart Preston station to Liverpool Lime Street station
1801 hours	Arrive Liverpool Lime Street station. Taxi to Thistle Liverpool Hotel, Chapel Street, Liverpool, L3 9RE. Accommodation booking reference: 7843983.
1930 hours	Mr Simon Brake, Northern Area Manager, will meet you in hotel reception. A table has been reserved in Café Rendezvous, the hotel restaurant.

>3LS
Sunday 16 February

0900 hours	Taxi to Liverpool Arena
1000–1230 hours	Attend final of 'Young Project Manager of the Year' at the Liverpool Arena. Taxi to Lime Street station.
1322 hours	Train departs Liverpool Lime Street station to Pitlochry station

DON'T FORGET

Always leave plenty of room to allow the tear-off portion to be completed by hand – press the **return** key twice between each line or use double-line spacing.

VIDEO LINK

Learn more about business letters by watching the clip at www.brightredbooks.net

ONLINE TEST

Test yourself on business documents online at www.brightredbooks.net

 THINGS TO DO AND THINK ABOUT

Head to the digital zone to the folder called *Business Documents* for a number of exercises where you can practise your skills.

BUSINESS DOCUMENTS: MEETINGS DOCUMENTATION

When dealing with formal meetings, there is a specific procedure to be followed and particular documentation that has to be prepared.

NOTICE OF MEETING AND AGENDA

A **Notice of Meeting** lets everyone know why, when and where a meeting has been arranged. An **Agenda** is a list, in order, of topics to be discussed. These are often combined in the same document.

Example:

CARRON SPORTS COMMITTEE   Make use of bold to highlight headings

>3LS

A meeting of the Carron Sports Committee will be held in the Main Conference Room on Monday 18 April 2015 at 2030 hours.

>3LS   Always include the type of meeting, the venue, the date and the time

AGENDA

>2LS

1. Apologies
2. Minutes of the last meeting
3. Matters arising
4. Treasurer's report   These items may vary. Items highlighted in yellow are
5. Golf outing   standard items that appear on most Agendas
6. Cross country race
7. Any other business
8. Date of next meeting

MINUTES

It is important that all points raised in the meeting are noted so that a summary is recorded. **Minutes** reflect the Agenda and show who was present, what was discussed and agreed, and any action points, that is, what has to be carried out, by whom and, if relevant, by what deadline. They are usually written in the third person.

Example:

CARRON SPORTS COMMITTEE

>3LS

Minutes of the Carron Sports Committee meeting held in the Main Conference Room on Monday 18 April 2016 at 2030 hours.

>3LS   Always include the type of meeting, the venue, the date and the time

PRESENT

>2LS

Niall Armstrong (Chair)   Aileen McLean (Secretary)   Frank Wood (Treasurer)   James Marshall   Christine Brown

1. Apologies

   Apologies were received from Fraser Smith.

contd

2. Minutes of the Last Meeting

The minutes of the last meeting were taken as read, agreed and signed by the Chair

3. Matters Arising

There were no matters arising.

> These items may vary. Items highlighted in yellow are standard items that appear in most Minutes

4. Treasurer's Report

The Treasurer reported that annual subscriptions were now due and that members had received notification of payment options. Reminders will be sent to those who have not paid at the end of next month.

5. Golf Outing

James Marshall confirmed that all arrangements were in place for the trip which takes place on 4 June 2016 and that all those attending have now paid. The bus has been booked but times have to be confirmed. It was agreed that the bus will leave the main car park at 0900 hours and will return at 1730 hours approximately.

6. Cross Country Race

The date of the race has been confirmed as 31 July 2016. Posters advertising the event have now been prepared and entry forms are available from Christine Brown. All committee members should ensure that posters are displayed within their areas and they have a supply of forms.

7. Any Other Business

There was no other business.

8. Date of Next Meeting

It was agreed that the next meeting will be held on 19 May at 2030 hours.

Niall Armstrong
Chair

Action minutes

These record decisions reached and actions to be taken but not the discussion itself. They include a report of actions taken since the last meeting as well as planned actions. It is important to note who is responsible for upcoming actions.

ACTION MINUTES

Meeting of:	Carron Sports Committee	**Present:** Niall, Aileen, Frank, James, Christine
Venue:	Main Conference Room	**Apologies:** Fraser
Date:	Monday 18th April 2015	
Time:	2030 hours	

ACTION	WHO	DUE BY
Subscriptions		
Annual subscriptions are now due and most have been paid.		
Reminders to be sent to those who have not paid subscriptions.	FW	31 May 2015
Golf Outing		
Date confirmed as 2 June 2015. All those attending have paid.		
Bus departure and return times to be confirmed with bus company – leave main car park 0900 hours and return 1730 hours approx.	JM	1 June 2015
Cross Country Race		
Posters to be displayed and supply of entry forms to be kept in each department.	All	25 April 2015

THINGS TO DO AND THINK ABOUT

Head to the digital zone to the folder called *Business Documents* for a number of exercises where you can practise your skills.

 DON'T FORGET

Whenever you create or edit multi-page documents always ensure there is consistent formatting and spacing throughout.

DON'T FORGET

When specifying dates always include the year and only include day, month and year, for example, 1 March 2016. Never write the date in a format that includes the words 'the' and 'of'. For example, 'the 1st of March 2016' is not acceptable.

VIDEO LINK

Check out the clip at www.brightredbooks.net for more on business documents.

 ONLINE TEST

Head to www.brightredbooks.net to test yourself on business documents.

MAIL MERGE

Mail merge allows you to produce multiple letters, labels and envelopes using information such as names and addresses stored in a spreadsheet or database file. You will need a Word document (new or existing) and a recipient list (typically an Access database or Excel spreadsheet file).

The **Mailings** tab contains all the buttons, menus and commands you need.

Example:

The following letter is to be sent to all pupils whose details are stored in a database. * indicates where information from the database table **Students** is to be inserted.

Ref

Today's Date

*

Dear *

MID-TERM BREAK

I am writing to confirm that school closes on Friday 1 April 2016 at 2:30pm for Spring mid-term break and will re-open on Monday 18 April 2016 at 8:50am.

I would like to take this opportunity to wish you all a happy holiday.

Yours sincerely

Joan King
Headteacher

After creating the letter, go to the **Mailings** tab, click on **Select Recipients** and select **Use Existing List...** to find the file that has already been saved.

The **Select Data Source** box will open; here you can search your **Documents** folder for the database (or spreadsheet) file that contains the information you want to insert in the letter. Click **Open**.

The **Select Table** window opens and shows the tables, queries or worksheets available as the data source. Make your choice and click **OK**.

Use the **Insert Merge Field** drop-down menu to see the field names available from the chosen table/query/worksheet. At the appropriate points within the document, select the fields that will give the information required.

contd

Field names (*field codes*) will now be shown in the document. Click on *Preview Results* to show the information contained in the database table/query/spreadsheet.

MAILING LABELS

Mailing labels can be stuck to envelopes or packages to display the name and address of the recipient. Labels come on a continuous roll or on sheets. Using mailing labels can be an essential time-saver when sending large volumes of mail.

To merge information from another file onto mailing labels, start with a new document. Go to the *Mailings* tab and click *Start Mail Merge*. Select *Labels...* from the drop-down list.

Choose a suitable label layout from the list of label vendors and a product number. For example, Avery A4/A5 L7160 produces a sheet with three labels across the page and seven down. Click *OK*.

A grid appears on the page. This is based on a table so if the gridlines cannot be seen click on the *View Gridlines* button on the *Layout* tab of the *Table Tools* ribbon. On the *Mailings* tab use the *Insert Merge Field* button to select the fields to be included in the label.

Only the first label on the sheet will be set up – once you are happy with the layout click on *Update Labels* and all the labels will be populated.

Click on *Preview Results* to view all the information from the database that will be printed.

DON'T FORGET

You are often instructed to print one copy of your document showing *field codes* and one copy showing any one record to prove that you have completed a mail merge and that you have used the correct source.

DON'T FORGET

The forward and back buttons and start and end buttons available in the *Preview Results* group on the *Mailings* tab will let you move through all the records that will be merged with the document.

VIDEO LINK

Head to www.brightredbooks.net to watch a tutorial on mail merging.

ONLINE TEST

Test yourself at www.brightredbooks.net

 THINGS TO DO AND THINK ABOUT

Head to the digital zone to the folder called *Mail Merge* for a number of exercises where you can practise merging information from a database with a Word document.

TIPS FOR VIEWING AND EDITING YOUR DOCUMENT

DOCUMENT VIEWS

Word documents can be viewed in different ways, which is helpful when you are creating and editing text, particularly if you are editing the layout of long documents with multiple pages. To change the view go to **View** then the **Document Views** group to select the most appropriate view. Alternatively, you can change views using the status bar at the bottom right-hand side of your screen.

The most useful view is **Print Layout** which shows how the document will look when printed. This is useful for editing headers and footers, adjusting margins, working with columns and drawing objects and is normally the default view. When working in **Print Layout** it is a good idea to ensure that the ruler is displayed both horizontally and vertically. If you cannot see the ruler go to the **View tab** and **Show** group and select **Ruler** or click on the **View Ruler** button at the far right.

DISPLAYING FORMATTING MARKS

When in **Print Layout**, it's useful to see formatting marks. This helps you find problems with your layout and ensures you don't delete essential formatting by mistake.

To display formatting marks, click the **Show/Hide** button ¶ in the **Paragraph** group on the **Home** tab.

The most common formatting marks are:

This·sentence·has·one·space·between·each·word.·

This·sentence·has·one·space·between·each·word¶
¶
This·is·the·start·of·a·new·paragraph¶

- **Space characters** – inserted by pressing the space bar and represented by a raised dot:

- **Paragraph marks** – inserted by hitting the **Return** key at the end of a paragraph and represented by ¶:

- **Line breaks** (or **soft returns**) – inserted by holding **Shift** and hitting the **Return** key and represented by a right-angled arrow ↵. These allow you to key in text on the next line down without losing any of the formatting within the paragraph. For example, they are useful in numbered lists for creating another paragraph within the same number without moving onto the next number.

1.→ This·is·the·first·paragraph·of·item·1.↵
    ↵
    This·is·the·second·paragraph·within·item·1.··Now·to·move·to·item·2·press·the·**Enter**·key.¶
¶
2.→ ¶

- **Tabs** – inserted by pressing **Tab** and represented by an arrow →. They are often used for creating columns of text.

Name	→	Department →	Salary¶
John·Smith	→	Sales →	£10,000¶
Jean·Brown	→	HR →	£12,500¶

- **Pagination breaks** – these include:

----------Page Break----------

············Column Break············

==========Section Break (Next Page)==========

==========Section Break (Continuous)==========

Page Break is used to start a new page.

contd

Column Break shows where the next column should begin. Unless you are instructed otherwise, you must assess how many columns are needed and how they will look when finished.

Section Break lets you divide a document into sections, allowing you to apply formatting or layout options to each individual section.

ZOOMING IN AND OUT

You can change how much of your document you can see on the screen by using the **Zoom** slider on the status bar at the bottom right of your screen:

You can also choose a setting from the **Zoom** group on the **View** tab:

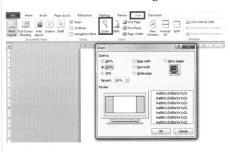

Zooming can be particularly helpful when editing the layout rather than the text as you can get an overview of where to split paragraphs, insert breaks and so on.

QUICK ACCESS TOOLBAR

You can add your choice of commands by selecting **More Commands...** which will take you into the **Word Options** dialog box. Ensure **All Commands** are visible then **Add** your selection and click **OK**.

You can move the **Quick Access Toolbar** to below the ribbon if you prefer.

FORMATTING TEXT

If you have spent time trying different combinations of fonts, sizes and colours for a particular piece of text, you can copy the formatting by using **Format Painter** on the **Home** tab, so that you can then apply it in other places. Select the text you have formatted, then click **Format Painter** – a single click will let you change one piece of text, double-clicking will change your cursor pointer to a paint brush 🖌 which can be used throughout the document. To turn off the format painter, press the **Esc** key or click the **Format Painter** button again.

THINGS TO DO AND THINK ABOUT

Head to www.brightredbooks.net to the folder called *Page Layouts* to practise.

🞤 DON'T FORGET

Section Breaks can be **Continuous** or **Next Page**. For more information about **Section Breaks** see pages 56–57.

🞤 DON'T FORGET

Formatting marks will only be displayed on your screen. They will not appear in your printed document.

🞤 DON'T FORGET

If you change the zoom setting and then save the document it will always open in that setting, but only if you have made other edits to the document.

🞤 DON'T FORGET

The **Quick Access Toolbar** at the top left of your screen is very useful for commands that you use very frequently – including undo ↶ which you can use if you accidentally delete a piece of text or make a mistake.

🞤 DON'T FORGET

A quick way to remove any formatting is to highlight the text then click on the **Clear Formatting** button in the **Font** group of the **Home** tab.

🞕 VIDEO LINK

Check out the clip at www.brightredbooks.net to learn more about editing Word documents.

LINE SPACING AND LISTS

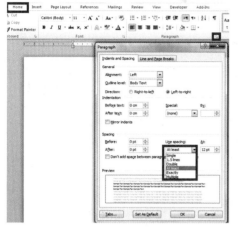

LINE SPACING AND PARAGRAPH SPACING

Line spacing is the amount of space between lines in a paragraph. It is typically based on the height of the characters, but can be changed to a specific value. It can be measured in **lines** or **points**. For example, when text is in **double line spacing**, the spacing is two lines high, meaning there is vertical spacing for the text plus the exact same amount of height space for the blank lines in between the lines of text. Alternatively, you might set 12-point text with 15-point spacing, which gives enough height for the text plus a little extra. You can reduce line spacing to fit more lines on the page, or increase it to improve readability.

Line spacing can be set using the **Paragraph** box which can be accessed from the expand arrow in the **Paragraph** group on the **Home** tab. If you select **At least** or **Exactly** from the drop-down menu beside **Line spacing**, it will be measured in points. Otherwise, it will be measured in lines.

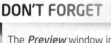

You can also set line spacing using the **Line and Paragraph Spacing** button on the **Home** tab.

Paragraph spacing is the space above or below a paragraph. Instead of hitting **Enter** several times to increase the space between paragraphs, you can set a specific amount of space before and/or after each one. It can be specified in the **Paragraph** dialog box or the **Paragraph** group on the **Page Layout** tab.

contd

DON'T FORGET

The **Preview** window in the **Paragraph** dialog box will show you the effects of any changes.

DON'T FORGET

The default settings in Word are 10-point spacing after the paragraph and 1·15 between lines. To save any of the formatting changes you make and automatically apply them to new documents click on **Set as Default** in the **Paragraph** dialog box.

DON'T FORGET

AutoCorrect Options will let you switch off bullets if you do not want them to be automatically created.

WORKING WITH BULLETED OR NUMBERED LISTS

Bulleted and numbered lists can be used in your documents to format, arrange and emphasise text. Word offers a variety of bullet options for customising lists:

Bulleted These have no significant order and are preceded by a symbol.
Numbered These have a sequence or priority and are preceded by a number or a letter.
Multilevel (outline numbering) These have numbers, bullets or a mix, and a hierarchy:
1   First level
   a)   Second level
      i)   Third level

Automatic bullets and numbers

Word can automatically create bulleted and numbered lists as you type. Start a paragraph with a hyphen (-) or an asterisk (*) or 1. then press **spacebar** or **tab** and then press the **Enter** key at the end of the line. Word will automatically convert the paragraph to a bulleted item and will continue to add to the list each time you press **Enter** at the end of a sentence. To finish the list either press **Enter** twice or press the **Backspace** key to delete the last bullet or number in the list.

Adding bullets/numbers to an existing list

Select the text you want to format as a list then click the **Bullets** or **Numbering** or **Multilevel List** drop-down arrow on the **Home** tab.

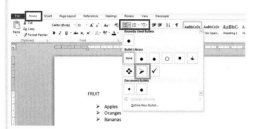

Select the bullet or numbering style you would like to use in the document.

To continue your list press the **Enter** key after the last item and the next bullet/number will be added. Bullets/numbering will continue each time you press the **Enter** key to start a new line in your list. When you have reached the end of your list, press the **Enter** key twice to return to 'normal' formatting.

To remove numbers or bullets from a list, select the bulleted/numbered list, then click the **Bullets** or **Numbering** buttons to switch them off.

To move the list across the page, select the list then click on the **Increase** or **Decrease Indent** buttons on the **Home** tab to move the list back to the left margin or further across the page to the right.

Alternatively, right-click with your mouse and select **Adjust List Indents...** In the **Adjust List Indents** dialog box you can specify exactly where the number or bullet will be placed in the document and how big the space will be between the bullet/number and the text.

HOW TO CHANGE NUMBER FORMATS

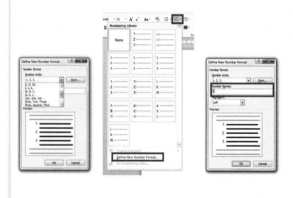

Click on the drop-down menu at the right-hand side of the numbering icon and the **Numbering Library** dialog box will open. You can select from the styles displayed or click on **Define New Number Format...** to open the **Define New Number Format** dialog box where you can select a **Number style** from a drop-down menu. The **Font...** button will let you change the font, font size, font colour and so on. Click **OK** to apply your choice.

Within the **Number Format** box further edits can be applied, such as removing the . after a number.

A list will automatically start at number 1 but you can change this by clicking on **Select Numbering Value...** from the drop-down menu from the **Number** icon . The **Set Numbering Value** dialog box will open where you can either **Start a new list** or **Continue from previous list**. Enter the first number to be used in the numbered list in the **Set Value To** box then click **OK**.

THINGS TO DO AND THINK ABOUT

Head to the digital zone to the folder called *Bullets & Numbering* for a number of exercises where you can practise your skills.

USING INDENTS AND TABS

Indents and **tabs** are tools for adding structure to a document and making it easier to read. A single word, line of text or entire paragraph can easily be moved to the desired location on a page.

Indenting text increases the space between the margin of the document and the text of the paragraph. Indents are usually from the left margin but can also be from the right.

The marker looks like one shape but it is in fact made up of three!

INDENT MARKERS

There are three indent markers at the start of the horizontal ruler that let you indent paragraphs from the left margin. They are:

- **First line indent** – indents the first line only, visually separating paragraphs. Hit *Tab* at the start of the paragraph to create a default indent of 1·27 cm.

- **Hanging indent** – indents every line except the first. Select the text then move the *Hanging Indent marker* to the desired location on the ruler.

- **Left indent marker** – select the text then click the bottom marker to move both the *First Line Indent* and *Hanging Indent* markers together and indent all lines.

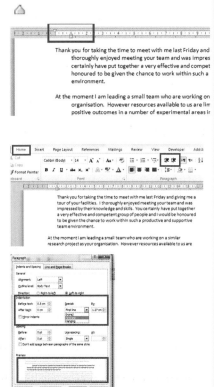

Alternatively you can use the *Decrease Indent* and *Increase Indent* commands on the *Home* tab to move the paragraph away from or towards the left margin.

You can also set the *Indent Left* and *Indent Right* measurements in the *Paragraph* group of the *Page Layout* tab.

Clicking on the expand arrow in the *Paragraph* group opens the *Paragraph* box. Here, specific measurements for indents can be set. *Preview* will show the effects of any changes.

Highlighting the text and moving the *Right Indent* marker at the right hand side of the ruler will increase the space between the paragraph text and the right margin.

TABS

Use **tabs** to control exactly where text is placed, especially when working with columns of text.

Every time the *Tab* key is pressed the insertion point will move 1·27 cm (default) to the right. By adding **tab stops** to the ruler you can change the spacing between tabs and have more than one type of alignment in a single line. For example, you can left-align the

contd

first column of the text, set a left tab stop at 7 cm then right-align the end of the line by setting a right tab at 16 cm.

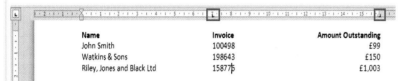

Name	Invoice	Amount Outstanding
John Smith	100498	£99
Watkins & Sons	198643	£150
Riley, Jones and Black Ltd	158775	£1,003

The tab selector

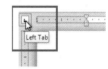

The **tab selector** is above the vertical ruler at the top left of the screen. Hover over the tab selector to see the name of the type of tab stop that is active. Types of tab stops include:

- **Left tab** – left-aligns the text at the tab stop
- **Centre tab** – centres the text around the tab stop
- **Right tab** – right-aligns the text at the tab stop
- **Decimal tab** – aligns decimal numbers using the decimal point
- **Bar tab** – draws a vertical line on the document

To add tab stops

There are two methods of inserting tabs into a document. For both, you must select the paragraph(s) you want to add tab stops to. If you don't, the tab stops will only apply to the text at that point in the document and any new paragraphs that you type below it.

Method 1 – click the expand arrow at the right of the *Paragraph* group in the *Home* tab. The *Paragraph* box will open, where you should select *Tabs...* to open the *Tabs* dialog box. Enter the ruler measurement for where you want the tab stop to appear as well as the alignment of the tab. Click *Set* then *OK*.

Method 2 – click the ruler at the top of the document. Click the tab selector above the vertical ruler in the top left-hand corner and keep clicking until the type of tab stop you wish to use appears. Move to the horizontal ruler and click the location on the bottom edge of the horizontal ruler where you want your text to appear and the tab stop to be set.

You can continue to add as many tab stops as you want.

THINGS TO DO AND THINK ABOUT

Head to the digital zone to the folder called *Tabs* for a number of exercises where you can practise your skills.

USING TABLES 1

A **table** is the obvious way to present information in rows and columns. Even if there are just a few rows of information, tables are easier to use than tabs and less likely to go wrong. You can align numbers and text in columns, sort the data and perform calculations.

CREATING TABLES

Word has options to create basic tables you can format yourself or you can choose from the built-in styles. There are three ways to create a table, all of which you can access from **Table** in the **Insert** tab.

1 Drag the cursor over the grid to select the required number of columns and rows.

2 Click on **Insert Table** and the dialog box opens. Specify the number of columns and rows needed. You can also select how the table will fit across the page by selecting a choice from **Autofit behavior** – have a look at the examples on the right:

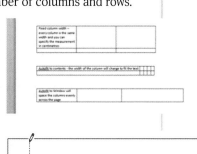

3 Click **Draw Table** . The cursor will change to a pencil, allowing you to draw the outer boundaries then the row and column lines inside.

Once your table has been created, the **Table Tools** toolbar becomes available – you can now choose either the **Design** or **Layout** tab.

Design tab

Here you can select pre-set **Table Styles** or you can select your own **Borders** and **Shading**.

Make sure you select the cells you want to format then the line style and weight before selecting the border that you want to change.

No Border will remove all printed borders from your table at once.

ONLINE

Head to www.brightredbooks.net to learn more about table properties.

Using the **Eraser** will take away any single lines not required.

To save time when designing a table, use one of the many pre-designed style formats within the **Table Styles** group (on **Design** under **Table Tools**). Selecting a style includes live preview which lets you see the effect of the style on the table.

The selections you make in **Table Style Options** determine how your table looks and what you see in the **Table Styles** gallery. For example, if you deselect **Banded Rows**, Word will not display styles with alternately shaded rows.

Layout tab

To change the structure of your table, use the buttons on the **Layout** tab under **Table Tools**. These will allow you to **Delete Cells**, **Merge Cells**, **Split Cells**, **Delete Rows** or **Insert Rows and Columns** as well as specify the width and height of cells and the alignment of text within the cells.

DON'T FORGET

As a quick alternative to splitting cells or merging cells you can click on either the **Draw Table** or **Eraser** icons on the **Design** tab to insert or remove lines.

Draw   Eraser
Table

BORDERS AND GRIDLINES

Borders are solid lines that are displayed when you print the document, while **gridlines** are only visible on screen as a means of showing you the structure of the table. By default all new table cells have black borders that show on the screen and which will be printed. If you remove the table borders by clicking on **No Border** (on the **Design** tab) you can still see where each cell is located by ensuring **View Gridlines** is selected on the **Layout** tab under **Table Tools**.

A useful command on the **Layout** tab is **AutoFit** in the **Cell Size** group. To fit a table neatly across a page, select **AutoFit to Window**. The table will then be resized to fit between the page margins.

DON'T FORGET

Remember table gridlines will not be printed but borders will.

DON'T FORGET

Row heights and width as well as text alignment and direction can also be changed using the commands in the **Layout** ribbon.

SELECTING ITEMS IN A TABLE

You may wish to make changes across all or part of a table. You may, for example, want to select the whole table to change the font, or to shade one cell only, or to put a border around some rows and so on. There are a variety of ways in which all or part of the table can be selected.

To select the entire table click on the table selector.

Alternatively use the **Select** button on the **Layout** tab for a list of options.

VIDEO LINK

Learn more about tables by watching the video at www.brightredbooks.net

ONLINE TEST

Test yourself on using tables at www.brightredbooks.net

THINGS TO DO AND THINK ABOUT

Head to the digital zone to the folder called *Tables* for a number of exercises where you can practise your skills.

USING TABLES 2

SORTING IN A TABLE

The ability to sort information within a table can be very useful. Select the area within the table that you want to include in your sort. Think carefully here! For instance in the table below, the TOTAL row should remain as the last row so it has been excluded from the selection.

In the *Layout* tab select the *Sort* button . Select which columns are to be sorted and in which order.

CONVERT TEXT TO TABLE

You may have a piece of text that has been laid out as a list that you want to put into a table in order to add some borders or shading.

Select the text and go to the *Insert* tab. Click on *Table* then *Convert Text to Table* and the dialog box will open. The number of columns and rows should be filled in automatically but ensure the choice made below *Separate text at...* reflects how the original text has been formatted, for example *Tabs* if the *Tab* key has been used to create columns.

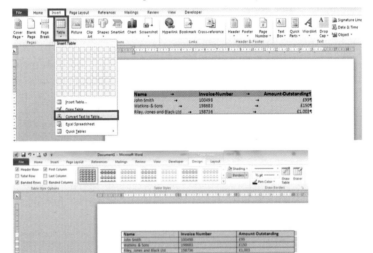

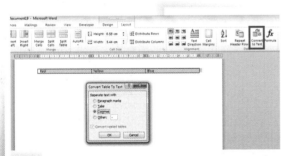

CONVERT TABLE TO TEXT

Select the table then select *Convert to Text*. There are a number of options to choose, for example *Commas* changes your table to a list using commas.

CALCULATIONS IN A TABLE

It is possible to carry out calculations within a table using any columns or cells that contain numbers or currency. The **Formula** command is found in the **Data** group on the **Layout** tab under **Table Tools**.

When you click on the **Formula** button, the **Formula** dialog box will open. Word defaults to a *Sum* calculation depending where you are in the table. For example, at the bottom of a column Word will suggest *=SUM(ABOVE)* or *=SUM(LEFT)* to calculate the total across a row. Using the drop-down list at **Number Format** you can select how you want your answer to be formatted, for example £ for currency.

Other formulae that use positional arguments (ABOVE, BELOW, RIGHT or LEFT) are:

=AVERAGE( ) finds the average of all values chosen
=COUNT( ) counts the number of values chosen
=MAX( ) finds the maximum value in the cells selected
=MIN( ) finds the minimum value in the cells selected.

Alternatively, you can enter your own formula. To do this you must imagine your table is an Excel spreadsheet – the only difference is that you cannot see the row and column headings. Always start your formula with = then key in the remainder of the formula as you would in a spreadsheet, making us of the +, –, / and * symbols where relevant.

You can format the result of your calculation as you did previously.

Updating a table

Once you have created your table and included formulae you can update calculations with any edits to figures by right-clicking your mouse whilst on the updated figure and selecting **Update Field**.

INSERTING DATA FROM EXCEL

Although Word includes the option of creating formulae in a table, sometimes it is easier to perform calculations in Excel and then copy and paste the data into your document.

Select the figures in the worksheet with your mouse then use the **Copy** and **Paste** icons in the **Home** tab to embed a copy of the Excel content in the Word file. This means that the information in the Word file will not change when the spreadsheet is modified.

ELECTRONIC FORMS

An **electronic form** is a special type of document in which you can only type your own information within certain areas – the remainder of the document is protected and cannot be modified. Customer survey questionnaires may, for example, be set up in this way. When working with this type of form, you can move directly between the answer boxes using the **Tab** key. As well as being able to type in your answers, you can also click on check boxes or select from pre-set answers provided in a drop-down list.

THINGS TO DO AND THINK ABOUT

Head to the digital zone to the folder called *Tables* for a number of exercises where you can practise your skills.

DON'T FORGET

The # sign within any of these formats will give additional spaces – these can be deleted so that all figures are consistently formatted.

DON'T FORGET

You cannot point and click with your mouse nor can you fill down so this means that every formula must be keyed in as you go down a column or along a row.

ONLINE

To learn about linked objects, head to www.brightredbooks.net

VIDEO LINK

Check out the clip at www.brightredbooks.net for more on this topic.

ONLINE TEST

Test yourself on using tables at www.brightredbooks.net

WORKING WITH STYLES

Headings can be used within a document to give structure and to make it easier for the reader to make sense of the content. Headings are often formatted differently from the main body of text to make them stand out, for example they might have a slightly bigger font size or be in bold. Rather than selecting each heading text and applying attributes – font, size, style and so on – you should use **Styles** to format text quickly and easily.

VIDEO LINK

Head to www.brightredbooks.net and check out the clip on this topic.

ONLINE TEST

Test yourself on formatting at www.brightredbooks.net

USING STYLES

A **Style** is a predefined set of formatting specifications that can include both font and paragraph settings. When you apply a **Style**, Word formats the text according to how the **Style** has been defined.

There are a number of benefits to be gained from using **Styles**:

- consistency – text is formatted in the same way throughout the document
- ease with which the formatting can be changed – simply modify the **Style** once in the **Styles** group and all the text formatted with that particular style will change
- access to time-saving features – you can make use of automatic functions, such as tables of contents, navigation pane, heading numbering and so on

Styles and navigation

If you have used **Styles**, you can use the **Navigation** pane to move around your document quickly. Clicking on a heading in the **Navigation** pane will take you directly to that location within the document. You can also reorganise your document easily by dragging and dropping entire sections.

To display the pane, click on the **View** tab and select **Navigation** pane in the **Show** group.

Word includes a range of built-in **Styles**. There are two main types:

Paragraph – applied to an entire paragraph. As well as text formatting, this style includes paragraph formatting such as spacing and alignment. Paragraph styles are indicated by the symbol ¶.

Character – applied to selected text. This style includes font formatting only, for example, italic, bold or underline. Word indicates character styles with the symbol **a**.

Some **Styles** are a combination of paragraph and character formatting.

Applying a style using the **Quick Styles** gallery

Word displays the most commonly used styles in the **Styles** group on the **Home** tab. Using the scroll bar will display more styles.

DON'T FORGET

Normal is Word's default paragraph style which means that this is the **Style** that is normally used when you start a new Word document.

The quickest way to apply **Styles** to your text is to highlight the text and click on the name of the **Style** you want to apply. For our purposes we would normally choose **Heading 1** for main headings, **Heading 2** for sub headings, **Heading 3** for sub sub headings and so on.

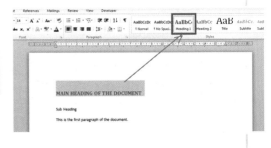

contd

To view all styles available in Word

Click on the expand arrow at the right-hand side of the **Styles** group to open the **Styles** pane.

To ensure that you see all the **Styles** within the **Styles** pane that Word has to offer click on **Options** at the bottom of the pane. The **Style Pane Options** dialog box will open and you can then choose **All Styles** from the drop-down menu and click **OK**.

To modify styles

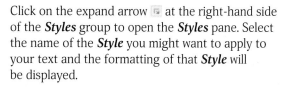

Click on the expand arrow at the right-hand side of the **Styles** group to open the **Styles** pane. Select the name of the **Style** you might want to apply to your text and the formatting of that **Style** will be displayed.

To make modifications to that **Style** click on the drop-down menu beside the **Style** name and select **Modify**.

The **Modify Style** window will open where you can change the font, size and so on. Click on the **Format** button within this menu to make further changes. Remember to click **OK** when you have made your selections.

By default, any changes you make to any of the **Styles** apply to the current document only. If you want the changes to apply to every new document you create, click on **New documents based on this template** in the **Modify Style** dialog box. Be careful to use this option with caution – some formatting you may not want in every document!

To create a new style

One of the easiest ways to create a new **Style** is to format a piece of text with the font, font size and format which you want as a new **Style**.

Key in two words and set up the format, for example, Arial, 14-point size, bold and italics.

Select the words with the mouse. Right-click the selection and select **Styles** from the drop-down menu. Click **Save Selection as a New Quick Style...** and this will open the **Create New Style from Formatting** dialog box.

Choose a name for your new style and then click **OK**.

The new style that you have created now appears in the **Quick Styles** gallery with the name you gave it and is ready to be used.

To create a new style without applying it to text, first click on the expand arrow at the right-hand side of the **Styles** group to open the **Styles** pane. Click on the **New Style** icon at the bottom of the **Styles** box.

The **Create New Style from Formatting** dialog box will open and the font, font size and so on can be chosen for the new style. Give the new style a name and click on **OK**.

THINGS TO DO AND THINK ABOUT

Head to www.brightredbooks.net to the folder called *Styles* for a number of exercises where you can practise your skills.

TABLE OF CONTENTS, MARGINS AND PAGE ORIENTATION

CREATING A TABLE OF CONTENTS

If you are working with a large document such as a report, the final stage, once all text has been edited, graphics inserted, page numbers added and so on, is to create a **table of contents**. The benefit of using *Styles* is that you can do this automatically – Word will use the text that has been formatted with *Styles* to build the table. For example, if you have used *Heading 1*, *Heading 2* or *Heading 3* to format any of the headings throughout your document, Word will pick these up and match them with their correct page number.

A table of contents is normally inserted on a separate page within a large document and is very often the second page after a front cover.

Go to the *References* tab and select *Table of Contents*. To keep it simple, choose either *Automatic Table 1* or *Automatic Table 2*. The table of contents will now be created.

In the *Table of Contents* menu, clicking on *Insert Table of Contents...* will open the *Table of Contents* dialog box where the format of the leader dots can be changed or removed altogether. If you have used more than three heading styles you can select or change the number of levels that are picked up by using the up/down button at *Show levels*.

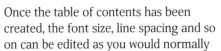

Once the table of contents has been created, the font size, line spacing and so on can be edited as you would normally in a Word document – highlight the text within the table of contents and either right-click with your mouse or use the buttons on the toolbar.

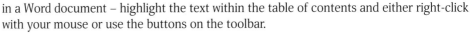

Updating tables of contents and page numbers

If changes are made to the document after the table of contents has been inserted, such as adding new pages or new headings, it will have to be updated. Either click at the top of the table of contents and then click ▣ Update Table... or select *Update Table* from the *References* tab.

From the *Update Table of Contents* prompt, you can *Update the page numbers only* or *Update entire table*. It is always a good idea to update the entire table.

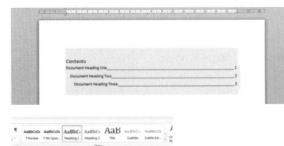

DON'T FORGET ⊕

A table of contents can also be used to navigate around your document on screen. Go to the table of contents and hold down the *Ctrl* key, then click on the heading where you want to be taken to. The heading will change to a hyperlink and take you to that page.

contd

MARGINS AND PAGE ORIENTATION

The margins and page orientation of a document can be altered in two ways. The easier way is to go to the **Page Layout** tab and select the appropriate icon.

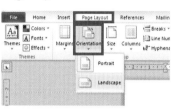

Alternatively, click on the expand arrow at the right-hand side of the **Page Setup** grouping on the **Page Layout** tab and the **Page Setup** dialog box will appear.

Under the **Margins** tab you can alter margins to the measurements you want as well as specifying whether you want the orientation of your page to be **Portrait** or **Landscape**.

To alter the vertical alignment of the text on your page, select the **Layout** tab then use the drop-down arrow at **Vertical Alignment** to make your choice.

Columns

Columns are used in many types of documents, such as newspapers and magazines.

Select the text you want to format or open a new document and click on **Columns** on the **Page Layout** tab. The number of columns required can be chosen from the drop-down menu. Choosing **More Options** will open the **Columns** dialog box and allow you to determine the width of the columns, the amount of space between columns and whether you want the columns separated with a vertical line.

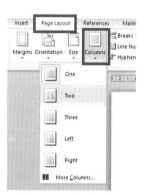

To remove the columns just click the **Columns** command and select **One** for the number of columns.

DON'T FORGET

If your table of contents doesn't work, go back and make sure you have formatted all the relevant headings within your document using **Styles** from the **Styles** gallery in the **Home** tab.

DON'T FORGET

Selecting **Custom Margins...** from the **Margins** drop-down menu will also open the **Page Setup** dialog box.

VIDEO LINK

Check out the clip about this topic at www.brightredbooks.net

ONLINE TEST

Test yourself on formatting at www.brightredbooks.net

THINGS TO DO AND THINK ABOUT

Head to www.brightredbooks.net to the folder called *Table of Contents* for a number of databases where you can practise your skills.

BREAKS

INSERTING BREAKS

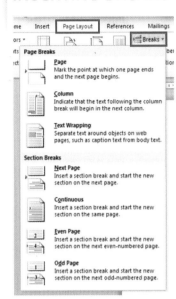

Word will automatically move on to a new page when text reaches the end of a page. You can, however, insert a **break** at any point in the document if you want more control over the formatting and layout of the text.

Word has several different types of breaks to choose from. They can be found on the drop-down menu beside *Breaks* on the *Page Layout* tab. Each type of break serves a different purpose and will affect the document in a different way. *Breaks* are divided into *Page Breaks* and *Section Breaks*.

Page breaks

Page – moves text to a new page before reaching the end of a page.

Column – if the document is formatted with columns, the text will automatically flow from one column to the other. Inserting a *Column break* will move text into the next column at that point.

Text Wrapping – This type of break is intended for use with text that wraps around graphics, tables and so on. The line of text is broken and then continues on the next line below the picture.

Section breaks

These create a barrier between parts of the document for formatting purposes and allow you to create different types of page-specific formatting within the same document. Each section can contain unique page numbering, margin sizes, headers and footers, and page orientation.

There are four different types of *Section Breaks*:

Next Page – inserts a section break so the new section begins at the top of the next page.

Continuous – inserts a section break on the same page. Use this if you want different formatting on a single page, such as columns in one section and margin-to-margin text in another.

Even Page – inserts a section break and starts the section on the next even-numbered page in the document.

Odd Page – inserts a section break and starts the section on the next odd-numbered page in the document.

You will probably find that most of the time you will use either a *Page Break* when you want a new page or a *Next Page Section Break* when you want to change the layout of one or two pages in the middle of a document.

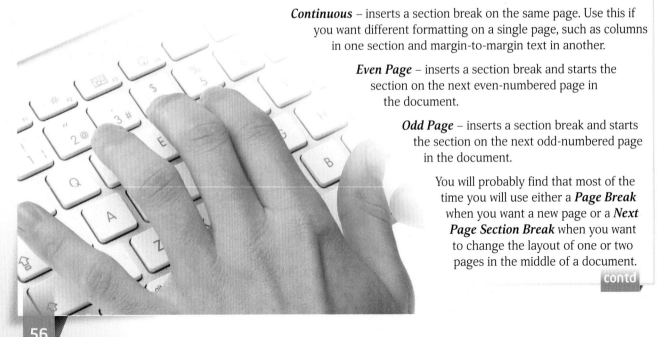

contd

Here is an example of how a **Next Page Section Break** can be used to change the page orientation from portrait to landscape and back to portrait in a single document.

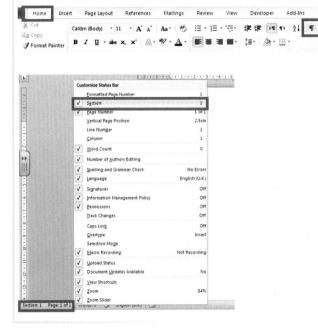

THINGS TO DO AND THINK ABOUT

You can customise the *status bar* at the bottom of the screen to display the number of the section you are working on so that you can keep track of where you are. Right-click the grey status bar and the *Customize Status Bar* menu will appear – select *Sections*. You can also choose to display the page number as shown on the page (*Formatted Page Number*), as well as the physical *Page Number*.

DON'T FORGET

Normally you cannot see *Breaks* on your screen, so if you want to check them, go to the *Home* tab and click the *Show/Hide ¶* command.

DON'T FORGET

To delete a *Page Break* select it by clicking in the margin next to the dotted line then press the *Delete* key on your keyboard.

DON'T FORGET

When you delete a *Section Break*, you also delete the section formatting for the text before the break. That text becomes part of the following section, and it assumes the formatting of that section. For example, if you have a five-page document with section breaks at the top of pages two and five, the section break on page two controls the formatting on page one and the section break at the top of page five controls the formatting for pages two, three, and four.

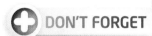

VIDEO LINK

For more on breaks, watch the clip at www.brightredbooks.net

ONLINE TEST

Test yourself on this at www.brightredbooks.net

USING HEADERS AND FOOTERS

Headers (top of a page) and **footers** (bottom of a page) can be used to display text or **fields** (which will automatically update).

By default, content entered in a header or footer appears on every page. However, **Section Breaks** allow you to change the header and footer for each section. For example, different text can be inserted on different pages or page numbering can be shown only on selected pages. This is done by unlinking headers/footers and formatting them separately. For example, each of these pages has a different header and footer – the text is different and the alignment varies:

To insert a header or footer go to **Insert** and select either **Header** or **Footer**.

Both have a number of **Built-In** styles to choose from which offer a variety of layouts. Choosing a **Built-In** style means that you do not have to manually amend the header/footer layout if the layout of any part of the document changes.

If, however, you have not used a **Built-In Header** or **Footer style** and have changed the orientation or margins for one part of your document there is still the option of resetting the tabs automatically by clicking on the **Insert Alignment Tab**. The **Alignment Tab** dialog box will open allowing you to change the alignment. It is worth noting that whilst the text is now aligned as selected, the tab marker on the ruler has not actually changed.

Once either a Header or Footer has been inserted, the **Header and Footer Tools Design** tab will appear on the ribbon which will let you insert the page number, date and so on.

Select **Different First Page** to alter the header or footer of the first page of a document. Use this command when the first page is the only different header or footer you want in the document; otherwise, use **Section Breaks**.

CREATING DIFFERENT SECTION HEADERS AND FOOTERS

When you create a new section it is linked to the previous section by default and the content and formatting of headers and footers continues. If you are editing the header or footer, you will see the label `Same as Previous` on the right and in the *Navigation* group, *Link to Previous* will be highlighted.

To make a different header or footer you must unlink it so click on *Link to Previous* and the link will now be broken. It is important to note that headers and footers are linked and unlinked independently. Although you unlinked the header, you still have the choice to unlink the footer too.

Inserting page numbers

The most straightforward method of inserting page numbers is to open the header or footer and place your cursor where you want the page number to appear.

In the *Header and Footer* group, click on *Page Number*, then select *Current Position* and choose *Plain Number*.

Once you have inserted the page number it may need to be formatted to ensure it is starting at 1 in the right place. Click on *Page Number* again and select *Format Page Numbers*. Either select *Continue from previous section*, which allows page numbers to continue, or click on *Start at* to specify the page number.

To separate the header/footer from the text

To separate the header or footer from the main part of the document by a line running from margin to margin, use the *Border* button on the *Home* tab and select *Bottom Border* when in the header and *Top Border* when in the footer.

To remove a header or footer

Click on either the *Header* or *Footer* button on the *Header & Footer Tools Design* tab and select *Remove Header* or *Remove Footer*.

THINGS TO DO AND THINK ABOUT

Head to www.brightredbooks.net to the folder called *Headers and Footers* for a number of exercises where you can practise your skills.

WATERMARKS, COMMENTS, FOOTNOTES AND ENDNOTES

WATERMARKS

A **watermark** is a piece of text or an image that is inserted behind document text to make it more visually interesting or to show the status of the document (for example, 'Confidential'). Text watermarks can be added from a gallery. Alternatively, you can create your own custom watermark – either your own text, a company logo or a graphic.

Watermarks are visible in *Print Layout* and *Full Screen Reading* views or on a printout of the document.

To insert a text watermark on all pages of the document

On the *Page Layout* tab, click *Watermark*.

Scroll through the gallery for predesigned watermarks. To key in your own text select *Custom Watermark...*. Click *Text watermark* and key in your text. You can also use this box to format the watermark. Click on *Apply*.

To turn a picture into a watermark

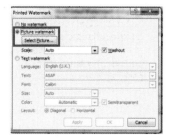

The *Printed Watermark* dialog box allows you to use a graphic. Click *Picture watermark* then *Select Picture*. You can then select a picture you have already saved and click *Insert*.

The size can be changed from the *Scale* drop-down menu or lightened using the *Washout* check box.

To insert a watermark on selected pages only

First, you must separate the document into sections. Click the *Show/Hide* ¶ button in the *Paragraph* group on the *Home* tab to see page breaks. Replace them with *Section Breaks (next page)*.

Watermarks normally appear in the centre of a page, however Word places them in the *Header*. The **links** between headers in different sections can be broken so the watermark only appears in the sections you want. In the document shown below the link between Header – Section 1 and Header – Section 2 has been broken, as has the link between Header – Section 2 and Header - Section 3. This means that Header – Section 2 is now totally on its own and therefore the watermark can be inserted just in the header of that section.

To modify or remove a watermark

To modify the existing watermark click on *Watermark* and select *Custom Watermark*. The *Printed Watermark* box opens, showing the settings of the current watermark for editing.

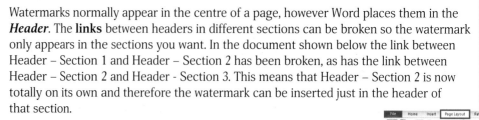

Delete the watermark from the document by clicking *Remove Watermark* in the same window.

You can also double-click in the *Header* of that section to edit or remove the watermark.

COMMENTS

Comments are like yellow sticky notes and are a way of making notes without changing the original text or impacting the printed version. They may be included to give editing instructions.

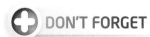

To add a comment, click immediately after the relevant word, then, in the *Review* tab, click *New Comment*. The *Comment* area opens to the right of the text with a dotted line leading to the section of text being commented on. Click in the *Comment* area and type your comment. When you have finished the comment click back in the document.

To delete a comment, click on it. In the *Comments* group in the *Review* tab click *Delete*. There is also the option to *Delete All Comments in Document* which means that you can action each comment as you work through the document, go back and double-check all instructions have been carried out then delete all the comments at the same time.

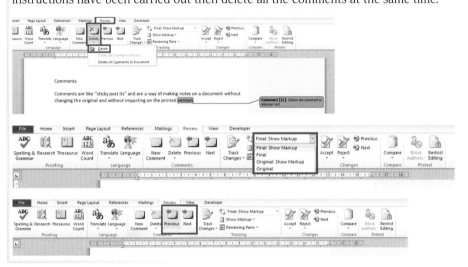

DON'T FORGET

Comments will pick up the initials of the user adding the comment and will be numbered sequentially.

DON'T FORGET

The document can be viewed with or without the comments showing. In the *Review* tab select either *Final: Show Markup* to see the comments or *Final* to keep them hidden.

DON'T FORGET

Also in the *Comments* group of the *Review* tab are the *Previous* and *Next* buttons to help you move backwards and forwards between comments in a long document.

FOOTNOTES AND ENDNOTES

A **footnote** is an additional piece of information included at the bottom of the page. An **endnote** appears on the very last page of the document.

Put your cursor where you want to insert your footnote or endnote. From the *References* tab select *Insert Footnote* or *Insert Endnote*.

A reference mark (usually a number) will be inserted next to the word in the text and the same reference mark will appear next to the footnote/endnote. A separator line will also be inserted automatically to separate the footnote/endnote from the body of text.

To delete a footnote or endnote delete the marker in the body of text, not in the footnote or endnote. When a new footnote/endnote is inserted or deleted the numbers will automatically be updated to ensure they run sequentially.

To adjust any of the settings of the footnote or endnote, for example to change the marker from numbers to roman numerals or symbols, click on the expand icon in the *Footnote* group of the *References* tab. The *Footnote and Endnote* dialog box will open. Make the changes you want and click *Apply*.

THINGS TO DO AND THINK ABOUT

Head to www.brightredbooks.net to the folder called *Watermarks, comments and footnotes* for a number of exercises where you can practise your skills.

VIDEO LINK

Learn more about watermarks by watching the video at www.brightredbooks.net

USING WORD COUNT, SPELLCHECK, THESAURUS AND FIND AND REPLACE

Useful tools for working with text are *Word Count*, *Spelling and Grammar* and the *Thesaurus*.

WORD COUNT

Word Count counts all the words in a document. This is useful for written assignments which have a limited word total, such as a 600-word report.

Word Count can be found on the *Review* tab. Click this and a dialog box appears with document information including the number of words, pages, characters, paragraphs and lines.

DON'T FORGET

By default, the number of words in a document appears in the status bar at the bottom of your screen.

DON'T FORGET

To count the number of words in only a certain part of the document, select the text you want to include in the count. The number of selected words will appear in the status bar. If you want to select text from various parts of your document press the *Ctrl* key and select the nonadjacent text.

SPELLING AND GRAMMAR

The spelling and grammar tool helps you produce error-free professional documents. You can run a spelling and grammar check or you can let Word check automatically as you type.

To run a **spelling and grammar check**, go to *Review* and click on *Spelling & Grammar*. For each error Word will offer suggestions. You can select a suggestion and click *Change* to correct the error or you can key in the correct spelling and click *Change*.

You have to be very careful as Word may not pick up all the grammatical errors, or it may highlight something as an error which is in fact correct, for example people's names which are not in the dictionary. You can ignore both spelling and grammar 'errors' either once or every time that particular error appears. If a word is highlighted as an error but is in fact correct, you can add it to the dictionary – but make sure the word is spelled correctly before choosing this option!

DON'T FORGET

Check that the dictionary is using *English (U.K.)* rather than *English (U.S.)* – this can be changed in the *Spelling and Grammar* dialog box using the drop-down menu at *Dictionary Language*.

Most of the time Word will automatically check your document for spelling and grammar errors and you may not need to run a separate spelling and grammar check. There errors are indicated by coloured wavy lines: red shows a word has been misspelled; green indicates a grammatical error and blue shows a contextual spelling error (when a word is spelled correctly but used in the wrong context, for example 'I don't no what to do next').

DON'T FORGET

Pressing the *F7* key on your keyboard will also run a spelling and grammar check!

When an error shows, right-click on it and a menu will appear. Click the correct spelling of the word to correct it. Alternatively you can choose to *Ignore* or *Add to Dictionary*.

contd

Similarly, with a grammatical error, you are given suggestions which you can choose to accept or *Ignore*. Go to *Grammar* or click *About This Sentence* for information on the rule.

The automatic settings can be changed in the *File* menu (select *Options* then *Proofing*).

THESAURUS

Word's built-in **thesaurus** helps you find synonyms for a word. For example, you can use the thesaurus to replace the word 'good' with one of its synonyms, such as 'decent' or 'suitable'.

Select the word, click *Review* and then *Thesaurus*. The *Research* pane appears with suggestions. Click the drop-down menu beside the replacement and select *Insert*.

Alternatively, right-click the word and point to *Synonyms*. Either accept a suggestion or select *Thesaurus* and the *Research* pane will open.

FIND AND REPLACE

You may wish to **find** a specific word or phrase within a document. Word can search the document using the *Find* feature and will also allow you to change a word or phrase using *Replace*.

Click the *Find* command. This opens the *Navigation* pane.

Key in the text in the field at the top of the navigation pane. If it is in the document, it will be highlighted in yellow, and a preview will appear in the *Navigation* pane. If it appears more than once, click the arrows on the *Navigation* pane to progress through the results. You can also click the *Result Previews* on the *Navigation* pane to jump to the location of a result in your document. When you close the *Navigation* pane, the highlighting will disappear.

If you want to replace text, from the *Home* tab click the *Replace* command.

Type the text you want to search for in the *Find what* field then type the replacement text in the *Replace with* field.

Click *Find Next* and then *Replace* to replace text. You can also click *Replace All* to replace all instances within the document.

 THINGS TO DO AND THINK ABOUT

Head to www.brightredbooks.net to the folder called *Word Count & Spellcheck* for a number of exercises where you can practise your skills.

SPREADSHEETS

RELATIVE AND ABSOLUTE CELL REFERENCES, NAMED CELLS AND RANGES

Spreadsheet software, such as Excel, should be used to carry out mathematical calculations, to analyse numerical data or to present information graphically in the form of a chart.

RELATIVE AND ABSOLUTE CELL REFERENCES

Calculations carried out in a spreadsheet use **formulae** based on the **cell references** (**addresses**) of the data to be included in the calculation.

Cell references can either be **relative** or **absolute**. Relative and absolute references behave differently when copied and filled to other cells:

- Relative cell references change when a formula is copied to another cell in the worksheet.
- Absolute cell references remain constant and will not change when they are copied to another cell in the worksheet.

In this worksheet, to calculate the total value of sales for each item listed, you need to multiply the quantity (column B) by the price (column C). For the first item in the list, this formula is written as **=B4*C4**.

The same calculation is used for all items so the formula created in cell D4 can be copied down to the other rows using the fill handle in the lower right corner of cell D4. As it is copied down the formula will change depending on its row – B4 and C4 change to B5 and C5 then to B6 and C6 and so on. Because the cell references change in this way this is known as a relative formula.

However, there may be times when you do not want a cell reference to change when the formula is copied. The solution is to use an **_absolute cell reference_** to keep a row and/or column constant.

An **_absolute reference_** contains the dollar sign ($) in front of either or both the column reference and the row reference that should not change when the formula is copied:

- **$A2** means that the column will not change – when this cell reference is copied the row number **2** will change but the column reference will always be **A**.
- **A$2** means that the row number will not change but the column reference will become B or C or D and so on
- **$A$2** means that neither the column letter nor the row number will change – when copied this cell reference will always be A2. This is the type of absolute cell reference you are most likely to use.

In this spreadsheet you want to calculate the amount of VAT for each item. The VAT amount in cell B10 is the same for all items – this should not change when the formula is filled down the column.

As you key in the formula **=D4*** and click on cell **B10**, whilst it is still highlighted, press **F4** – the dollar signs will now be included in your formula. The completed formula will read **=D4*$B$10**.

Now when the formula is copied down the column, the cell reference D4 changes to D5 then D6 then D7 but cell B10 does not change.

NAMED CELLS

Cells in a worksheet are normally referenced according to their column letter and row number. However it is possible to change the name of a cell to make it more meaningful.

For example in this worksheet the VAT rate of 20 per cent is in cell B10.

To change the name of this cell, click in the *name box*, delete **B10** and insert the words **VAT_Rate** (note that the computer will not accept a space between words so use _) and press the *Enter* key.

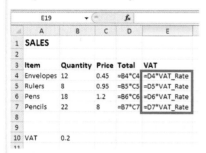

Now when the formula is inserted the name of the cell will be included and not the cell reference. When the formula is filled down the column, the named cell will remain unchanged – this is the same as using an absolute cell reference!

Named the wrong cell? Go to the *Formulas* tab then click on *Name Manager*. Select the name of the cell then click on *Delete*. You will be asked to confirm you want to delete the name, so do that and then click on *Close*. You can now select the correct cell to be named.

Note that within *Name Manager* there is also the option to *Edit* an existing name should you wish to change any spellings.

NAMED RANGES

It is also possible to name a range of cells so that they are easier to keep track of and so that formulae can be created more cleanly. Highlight the range and key in your chosen name in the *name box* as you would do with a single cell. For example, range **A3:B6** is now called **Price_List**. Named ranges are very useful when using VLOOKUPS and HLOOKUPS – see pages 68–71.

Any named cell or range of cells can easily be found by using the down arrow at the *name box* or by keying in the name that has been chosen. Clicking on the name will take you straight to that cell/range in the worksheet.

 THINGS TO DO AND THINK ABOUT

Head to www.brightredbooks.net to the folder called *Absolute & Named Cells* for a number of exercises where you can practise your skills.

 **DON'T FORGET**

Just as single cell references can be made absolute when included in a formula, so too can a range of cells. For example **$A$1:$C$4** means that this entire range of cells will not change when the formula is copied to another part of the worksheet.

DON'T FORGET

When reading task instructions to 'name the cell...' don't get confused. You should never name a cell containing text – you should only name cells containing numbers that you want to include in a formula!

DON'T FORGET

Using a *Named Cell* or a *Named Range* means that the cell or range is now fixed – this is the same as using an absolute cell reference.

DON'T FORGET

Rather than keying in cell references, you should always use your mouse to point and click on the cells you want included in formulae – that way you are less likely to make an error!

VIDEO LINK

Head to www.brightredbooks.net and check out the clips for more on cell referencing.

ONLINE TEST

Test yourself on this topic online at www.brightredbooks.net

MATHEMATICAL FUNCTIONS

COMMONLY USED FUNCTIONS

Spreadsheet calculations can be carried out in a number of ways. Straightforward addition, subtraction, multiplication and division can be inserted by starting with the = sign then pointing and clicking on the appropriate cells containing the numbers to be included in the calculations and inserting the appropriate mathematical operator: +, -, * and /.

For example, the formula to calculate the total in this spreadsheet is **=B4*C4**.

DON'T FORGET ➕

Use * for multiplication and / for division!

Other commonly used functions such as Average, Minimum, Maximum and so on are available using the down arrow beside the **AutoSum** button on the **Home** tab.

MORE COMPLEX CALCULATIONS

At Higher level you are expected to carry out calculations that are more complex. The **Insert Function** dialog box simplifies the task of using formulae in your worksheets and helps you locate the proper function for the task at hand as well as providing information about the arguments or conditions that the formula might include. If you use the **Insert Function** dialog box you do not have to type functions directly into worksheet cells. Instead, the dialog box guides you through mostly point-and-click steps that are similar to using a wizard.

The most common ways to do this are by clicking the **Insert Function** button on the **Formulas** tab **or** by clicking the **Insert Function** button (which looks like f_x) on the **Formula** bar.

You can also access the **Insert Function** dialog box by clicking the expand arrow at the bottom of the **AutoSum** button on the **Formulas** tab and selecting **More Functions....**

At Higher level the more advanced functions you are most likely to use are:

- ROUND
- ROUNDDOWN
- HLOOKUP
- COUNTIF
- ROUNDUP
- VLOOKUP
- IF
- SUMIF

ROUND, ROUNDUP and ROUNDDOWN

Numbers and text you enter in a spreadsheet can be formatted so that they automatically appear as currency, percentage, time and date and so on, and the number of decimal places displayed can be increased, decreased or specified exactly. These formatting options are available using commands in the **Number** group on the **Home** tab. Clicking the expand arrow will open the **Format Cells** dialog box making other formatting options available.

contd

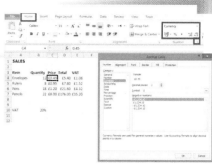

Rounding a number means giving a more approximate number when it is not necessary to be absolutely precise, for instance when estimating amounts of money, distances and so on. This makes the number easier to work with. However, it is very important to note that when you are instructed to round a number in a worksheet, you should not just change the formatting of the cell. Instead, you must use a formula as it is the underlying value in the cell that is being changed, not just the way it is being presented.

For example, this spreadsheet shows prices formatted as currency to two decimal places.

Round will round the number to the nearest specified number of decimal places. For example, 3·145 rounded to two decimal places will become 3·15. **Round Up** will force the number up so 3·145 will be 3·15. However **Round Down** will force the number down so 3·145 will become 3·14.

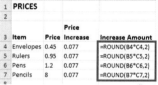

In this example, you want to increase prices by 7·7 per cent. The amounts shown are what the prices would look like before rounding. As you can see, it would be impractical to work with prices like these. To round to two decimal places click on f_x and select the **ROUND** function, and the **Function Arguments** dialog box will open.

The first line of the **ROUND Function Arguments** is the calculation that you want to carry out – in this example *Price x Price Increase* (B4*C4).

In the second line of the **Function Arguments** window specify the number of decimal places to which you want to round. Here it is two decimal places – note that a preview of the answer is shown. Click **OK**.

Copy the formula down the column as you would normally fill down. The price increases are now simpler and easier to work with.

When showing the worksheet in formula view it will be obvious that you have used the **ROUND function** and that you have not just changed the format of the cells to two decimal places.

ROUNDUP and **ROUNDDOWN** are carried out in exactly the same way – the first line contains the calculation and the second line contains the number of decimal places.

DON'T FORGET

Remember to use your mouse to point and click on the cells to be included in the calculation.

DON'T FORGET

Show Formulas is available on the *Formulas* tab.

VIDEO LINK

Explore this topic further by watching the clip at www.brightredbooks.net

ONLINE TEST

Test yourself on this topic online at www.brightredbooks.net

THINGS TO DO AND THINK ABOUT

To round to a whole number key in **0** and to round to the nearest ten key in **-1**. Notice also that the = sign is automatically given at the start of the formula – there is no need to key this in.

VERTICAL AND HORIZONTAL LOOKUPS

USING VERTICAL AND HORIZONTAL LOOKUPS

These are usually abbreviated to **VLOOKUP** for vertical lookup and **HLOOKUP** for horizontal lookup. Either type of lookup allows you to search for specific information in one part of a worksheet and receive an answer which is used in another part of the worksheet.

For example, imagine you have a price list of items in one part of your worksheet and you want to insert the prices from that list into your calculations in another part of the worksheet. You could copy the prices over or key them in individually but this would be time-consuming if you were using large, complex spreadsheets. In addition, if any prices change it is far quicker to locate the item in the price list than search through a large spreadsheet that might contain multiple entries relating to that item. In this situation a lookup should be used.

When do you use **VLOOKUP** and when do you use **HLOOKUP**? The answer depends on the way the information that will give you the answer has been laid out. In the 'GIFT SALES' example above, using the table of **CURRENT PRICES**, you have to first search vertically down the **Item** column to find the item you want, then find the price in the adjacent column – you would therefore use a **VLOOKUP**.

To find the corresponding grade for each pupil's mark in the 'EXAM MARKS' worksheet shown, you have to search horizontally along the first row of the **GRADES** table and then find the grade. This is an example of an **HLOOKUP**.

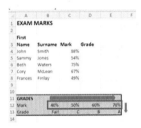

To create a lookup formula you must first ensure that you are in the cell where you want your first result to appear. (When you have completed the formula for the first item in the list you will then copy the formula down the column and find the information for the remaining items.) Now click on f_x and find either the **VLOOKUP** or the **HLOOKUP** function depending on the layout of the table of information.

The **Function Arguments** dialog box will open.

Both **VLOOKUP** and **HLOOKUP Function Arguments** dialog boxes have four lines – the first three lines are in bold, which indicates that each one must be completed with a piece of information; the last line is not bold and is therefore optional however it is best to get into the habit of entering either **TRUE** or **FALSE** .

Each line of the **Function Arguments** dialog box should be completed as follows:

Line 1

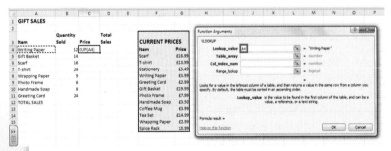

Lookup_value – What do you want to look up the value of? This is the first item in the list that you want to find the price of. In our example it is writing paper.

contd

Line 2

Table_array – Where will you get the value from?
This is the table of data you want to retrieve the information from. In this example it is the list of current prices of all the items. *LOOKUP* will always search the first column or row in this range, then it will return the answer from whichever column or row you specify. Do not include any header line and remember to make the table range absolute by pressing the *F4* key. Alternatively, before you begin the lookup you can give the table range a name so that when the *LOOKUP* formula is copied the cell references of this table will not change.

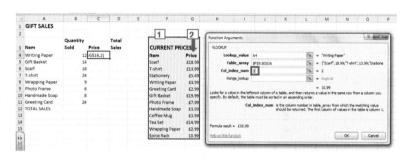

Line 3

In *VLOOKUP* this reads *Col_index_num* and in *HLOOKUP* this reads *Row_index_num*. Which exact column or row from the table of data highlighted will give you the answer? In this example the table of data is made up of two columns which were highlighted – you must look at this table only and ignore any other column or row references. The first column is the list of items; the second is the list of prices. Therefore the answer will come from the second column.

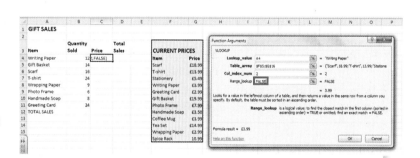

Line 4

Range_lookup – this will either be *TRUE* or *FALSE*. *FALSE* will look for an exact match of information – for example, writing paper in the list of items will match writing paper in the table of current prices. *TRUE* will look for the closest match but always below. This is used when dealing with a range of numbers – see the *HLOOKUP* worked example on the next page.

Finally click *OK*, check the formatting, then fill down the remainder of the column. The relevant information from the table of current prices will be added into the Price column.

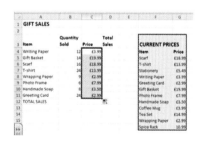

 THINGS TO DO AND THINK ABOUT

If the *LOOKUP* doesn't work check that there are no spelling errors or extra spaces in either in the data table or for the values you are looking up. This would result in no match. Also check that numbers have not been formatted as text. Finally check that you have used the *F4* key and made the cell references of the data table absolute so that when the *LOOKUP* formula is copied the cell references of the data table do not change.

DON'T FORGET

There are hints to help you work your way through each line of the *Function Arguments*.

VIDEO LINK

Check out the clip at www.brightredbooks.net to learn more about this.

ONLINE TEST

Test yourself on this topic online at www.brightredbooks.net

HORIZONTAL LOOKUP AND CONDITIONAL FORMULAE

HORIZONTAL LOOKUP

Example: *HLOOKUP*

In this example the grades of students should be inserted according to the mark they achieved. To find the grade you first have to look horizontally along the top row of the GRADES table then down to find the answer from the next row, hence the reason this is an **HLOOKUP**.

The first step is to click in cell **D4** where the first answer has to go, then insert the **HLOOKUP** function. The **Function Arguments** dialog box will open and each line can now be completed.

Line 1: **What do you want to look up the value of?** The mark of the first person in the list.

Line 2: **Where will you get the value from?** The table of data containing the grades. Remember: you should not include any headings and you must press the **F4** key to ensure that the cell addresses of the table become absolute and do not change when the formula is copied down.

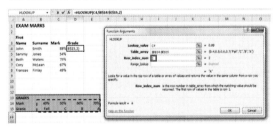

Line 3: **Which row from the table of highlighted data will the answer come from?** In this example, two rows in the table were highlighted. The first row is the list of marks; the second row is the list of grades. Therefore the answer will come from row 2. Remember – ignore the row numbers given in the worksheet and look only at the table of grades to find out which row will give you the answer.

Line 4: **Range_lookup** There is no exact match for any of the marks – they all fall within the ranges 40–50 per cent, 50–60 per cent or 60–70 per cent, and so the closest match will have to be found. Therefore this should be **TRUE**.

TRUE will look for the closest match but always below. John Smith's mark of 88 per cent will be matched to 70 per cent and will give the answer as A; Sammy Jones' mark of 54 per cent will be matched to 50 per cent and will give the answer C and so on. Note that when you are using TRUE, the values in the first row or column of the table containing the data must be sorted in ascending order otherwise you may not get the correct value. You will see the GRADES table in this example has been sorted from left to right in the ascending order of Mark. Finally, click **OK** and copy the formula down the column.

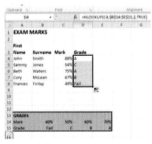

contd

CONDITIONAL FORMULAE

Excel has a number of functions that can be used to analyse data based on a condition.

SUM and SUMIF

When you want to total a column or row of numbers, either click directly on the **AutoSum** button on the **Home** tab or select the **SUM** function from the drop-down menu.

You may, however, only want to add a series of numbers that match specific criteria. In this example, if you want to add the total sales only for the Aberdeen Branch, then Aberdeen is your criterion.

Click on the cell where you want your answer to appear. Click on f_x and select the **SUMIF** function. The **SUMIF Function Arguments** dialog box will open.

Line 1: Range The area containing all possible matches for your criterion, in this case Aberdeen, is found in the column headed Branch, which is the range of cells B4:B18.

Line 2: Criteria The word or number that must be matched. In this case it is the word Aberdeen.

Line 3: Sum_range The range containing the numbers that you want added together if the criterion has been met.

Click **OK**.

Excel has looked through the list of branches to find Aberdeen and then summed the corresponding total sales figures.

In this example the range containing the Branch names does not change (B4:B18) nor does the range containing total sales (C4:C18). Therefore both these ranges should be fixed by pressing the **F4** key. Point and click on the first of the criteria, which is Aberdeen (cell A22), but leave this as a relative cell reference. When the formula to find the total for each of the branches is filled down from A22 the **Criteria** line will change to cell A23 (Perth) then cell A24 (Glasgow), then cell A25 (Edinburgh) and finally cell A26 (Dundee), but neither range will change.

 THINGS TO DO AND THINK ABOUT

Head to www.brightredbooks.net to the folder called *Vertical and Horizontal Lookups* for a number of exercises where you can practise your skills.

⊕ **DON'T FORGET**

When keying text in a spreadsheet formula remember to use double quotation marks " " around the word(s).

⊕ **DON'T FORGET**

It is sometimes possible to include the cell references of information included in the worksheet as part of the formula rather than keying in criteria separately. This means that you can fill the formula down the column and the criteria will change automatically. However, you must remember to make use of absolute cell references to ensure the ranges do not change when they are copied down.

CONDITIONAL FORMULAE AND IF STATEMENTS

CONDITIONAL FORMULAE

COUNT, COUNTA and COUNTIF

The **Count Numbers** function, which is available directly from the drop-down menu beside the **AutoSum** command on the **Home** tab, will count the number of numerical entries in a range. It is the same as the **Count** function, which is available from **More Functions...**

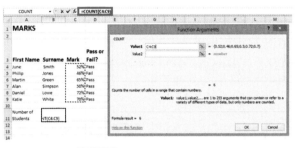

Using this function you can count the number of cells within a range that contain numbers.

To count cells containing text or words you must use the **COUNTA** function. Here the cells containing surnames can be counted.

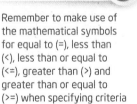

COUNTIF is used to count cells depending on a condition. In this example you want to count the number of students who have achieved a mark of less than 70 per cent.

Line 1 of the **COUNTIF Function Arguments** dialog box is the range that contains the criterion – in this example the list of marks in cells C4:C9.

Line 2 is the criterion that must be met – a mark <70 per cent.

The answer is four students.

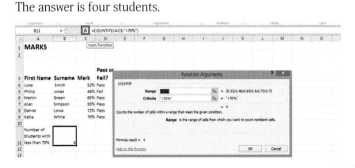

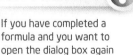

IF STATEMENTS

The **IF** function in a spreadsheet allows you to evaluate a situation which has two possible outcomes – there is a condition which must be met and there will be a different result depending on whether the condition is met (the statement is TRUE) or the condition is not met (the statement is FALSE).

In this example, the condition is that Sales Consultants earn commission on their total sales if their total sales are greater than or equal to £15 000. If this condition is met, then the statement is TRUE and the Sales Consultant will earn 20 per cent commission. If the condition is not met, however, then the statement is FALSE and the Sales Consultant will earn 0 per cent commission.

Sometimes it is easier to think of it as a 'yes' or 'no' answer to a question.

Example:

The **QUESTION** is: are total sales >=£15 000?
If the answer is **YES**: then 20% commission on total sales will be earned.
If the answer is **NO**: then 0% commission on total sales will be earned.

Let's put this into a formula. Click on where the answer will go for the first Sales Consultant on the list. Once the formula is complete it can be copied down the column to calculate the commission due to the remaining Sales Consultants.
Click f_x to open the **Insert Function** dialog box and select the **IF** function. The **IF Function Arguments** dialog box will open.

Line 1: Logical_test – this is the condition that has to be met. The question is are total sales >=£15 000?
Line 2: Value_if_true – what will happen if the condition in the first line is a true statement? If the answer to the question in Line 1 is yes then this is a TRUE statement and the Sales Consultant will get 20% of total sales.
Line 3: Value_if_false – what will happen if the first line is not a true statement? If the condition is not met then the answer to the question in Line 1 is no, this is therefore a FALSE statement and the Sales Consultant will get 0% of total sales. Click **OK**.

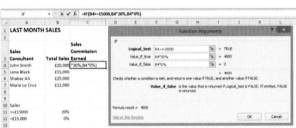

The final formula will read
=IF(B4>=15000,B4*20%,B*0%)

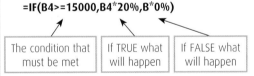

| The condition that must be met | If TRUE what will happen | If FALSE what will happen |

Note that the £ sign has not been included in the condition as this cell has been formatted for currency – the £ sign has not been keyed in.

 THINGS TO DO AND THINK ABOUT

Depending upon the layout of the worksheet it is possible to point and click and use cell references in the formula. However you must remember to use absolute cell references for those cells that do not change when you copy the formula down the column.

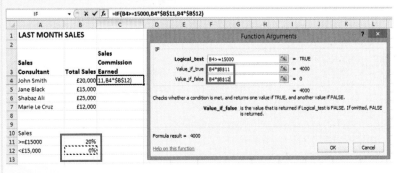

NESTED IF STATEMENTS AND CONDITIONAL FORMATTING

ONLINE TEST

Test yourself on this topic online at www.brightredbooks.net

DON'T FORGET

The third line of the wizard is either the final condition or it is the point at which you start a new IF statement.

DON'T FORGET

IF statements can be used to display text or carry out additional calculations depending on the conditions that have to be met. To return a 'blank' cell in an IF statement, key in " ".

DON'T FORGET

As you can see from the sales commission formula on the right, using nested IF statements can quite quickly get complicated. It is better not to try to key them in yourself – always use the **Function Arguments** dialog box if you can. You can have up to 64 IF functions nested in a formula but, as the formula can become very complex, it might be better to find a different way of doing things. Using the **VLOOKUP** function can sometimes be a better solution in a scenario like this.

DON'T FORGET

Remember you can use your mouse to point and click on relevant cells within your worksheet that can be used as part of the calculation – but remember to use absolute cell references!

NESTED IF STATEMENTS

Sometimes you need to work with situations where there are more than two possible outcomes. This is where multiple or **nested IF functions**, come in handy.

Example:

Sales Consultants earn commission on total sales as follows:
- total sales > = £20 000, commission is 30%
- total sales > = £15 000, commission is 20%
- any other amount of total sales (< £15 000), commission is 0% (that is, there is no commission)

Remember that the IF function works by evaluating a logical test to see whether it is TRUE or FALSE. It then includes a calculation if the logical test is TRUE, and another if it is FALSE.

Nested IF functions work by replacing one or both of the TRUE/FALSE calculations with another IF function. There are two rules you must follow when creating a nested IF statement:

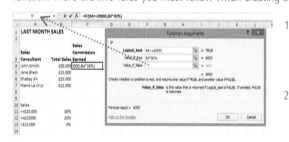

1 Start the IF statement with the highest condition that must be met – in this example the highest condition is total sales >=£20 000.

2 Put your cursor in the last line of the statement then click on IF to start a new statement containing the next condition – otherwise you will see a + sign in the middle of your statement and you will get an error. The **IF** statement will start again and you can enter the next highest condition – total sales >=£15 000 (remember not to key in the £ sign in the statement).

The last line of the **IF Function Arguments** will show the final condition. Here there are no other options – all Sales Consultants who achieve total sales <£15 000 will receive 0 per cent commission. Click **OK**.

The final formula will be
=IF(B4>=20000,B4*30%,IF(B4>=15000,B4*20%,B4*0%))

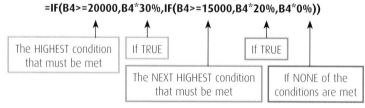

The HIGHEST condition that must be met | If TRUE | If TRUE

The NEXT HIGHEST condition that must be met | If NONE of the conditions are met

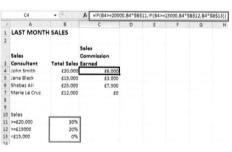

CONDITIONAL FORMATTING

Conditional formatting can be useful for highlighting information when data meets or fails to meet specific criteria. Conditional formatting allows you to apply formatting to one or more cells based on the value of the cell. You can highlight interesting or unusual cell values, and visualise the data using formatting such as colours, icons and data bars.

Conditional formatting applies one or more rules to any cells you want. An example of a rule might be **If the value is greater than £35 500, colour the cell green**. By applying this rule to the cells in a worksheet, you will be able to see at a glance which cells are more than £35 500. There are also rules that can mark the top ten items or mark all cells that are below the average or mark cells that are within a certain date range and many more.

Select the cells you want to add formatting to and go to the **Home** tab and within the **Styles** group click on **Conditional Formatting**. A drop-down menu will appear. Select **Highlight Cell Rules**.

A further menu will appear with several rules.

Once you have chosen the rule you want to apply, a dialog box will open where you can enter the appropriate value and select either a preset colour choice or **Custom Format...** which will allow you to choose the exact formatting you want.

The formatting will be applied to the selected cells.

Additional rules can be added. For example, imagine you now want to format all values less than or equal to £25 500.

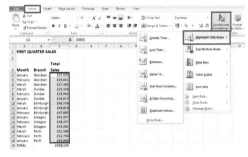

VIDEO LINK

Learn more about conditional formatting by watching the clip at www.brightredbooks.net

Click on **More Rules...** and the **New Formatting Rule** dialog box will open where again you can make your choices as to the rule to be applied as well as the formatting.

To remove conditional formatting rules

Select the cells that have conditional formatting. Go to the **Home** tab and click the **Conditional Formatting** command. A drop-down menu will appear where you can select **Clear Rules**. A menu will appear where you can choose to clear rules from the **Selected Cells** or the **Entire Sheet**.

Modify conditional formatting

You can edit or delete individual rules by clicking the **Conditional Formatting** command and selecting **Manage Rules**. The **Conditional Formatting Rules Manager** dialog box will open where you can add **New Rules...**, **Edit Rules...** or **Delete Rules**. This is especially useful if you have applied multiple rules to the cells.

 THINGS TO DO AND THINK ABOUT

Head to www.brightredbooks.net to the folder called *If Statements and Conditional Formatting* for a number of exercises where you can practise your skills.

SORTING AND FILTERING DATA

SORTING DATA WITHIN A SPREADSHEET

Data can be arranged to help you find it easily. Be careful, however, not to sort the data in only one column, as this can result in data mismatches.

To ensure this does not happen, drag your mouse over all the information you want included in your sort. Column headings become the **data headers**.

On the **Data** tab click **Sort**. Ensure that **My data has headers** is ticked. The computer will automatically deselect that row from the area to be sorted.

From the drop-down list you can now select the column you want to **Sort by**.

Sort On should be set as **Values** and **Order** can be set as **A to Z**, **Z to A** or **Custom List...** Click **OK**.

Sorting on multiple columns

Click on **Add Level** and, again, choose which column to sort on and in which order.

You can add a third level if you wish to sort on a third field, in the order of **Sort by**, **Then by**, **Then by**. Here the sort will be by branch and then, within branch, total sales will be sorted. To change the priority use the **Move Up** or **Move Down** arrows to re-order the list.

The **Sort** box is available on the **Home** tab using the **Sort & Filter** button and selecting **Custom Sort...**

Sorting horizontally

In the example, names have to be sorted into ascending order from left to right but the month column has to remain at the left of the worksheet.

Select the columns to be sorted with the mouse, remembering not to include column A, and click on **Sort** on the **Data** tab. Click **Options** where you can select **Sort left to right** and then click **OK**.

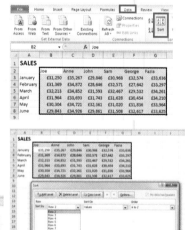

SALES						
	Joe	Anne	John	Sam	George	Fazla
January	£31,250	£35,267	£29,846	£30,968	£32,574	£33,636
February	£31,369	£34,872	£28,646	£32,571	£27,642	£33,297
March	£32,213	£34,852	£31,593	£32,467	£29,532	£34,261
April	£31,964	£33,693	£31,743	£31,628	£30,454	£34,210
May	£30,304	£34,721	£32,361	£31,020	£31,836	£33,964
June	£29,843	£34,926	£29,861	£31,508	£32,617	£33,625

Select the **row** with column headings to be sorted and click **OK**. The columns will change position and the names will now be sorted alphabetically.

SALES						
	Anne	Fazla	George	Joe	John	Sam
January	£35,267	£33,636	£32,574	£31,250	£29,846	£30,968
February	£34,872	£33,297	£27,642	£31,369	£28,646	£32,571
March	£34,852	£34,261	£29,532	£32,213	£31,593	£32,467
April	£33,693	£34,210	£30,454	£31,964	£31,743	£31,628
May	£34,721	£33,964	£31,836	£30,304	£32,361	£31,020
June	£34,926	£33,625	£32,617	£29,843	£29,861	£31,508

FILTERING DATA

Filtering is a quick and easy way to find and work with specific data and hide parts of it from view. You can use **AutoFilter** options or create your own filters. Unlike sorting, filtering simply hides the rows you do not want to see, letting you edit, format, chart and print the filtered data as you wish.

contd

To use filtering you must ensure that the top row of each column has a heading.

Using AutoFilter

Click on any cell then on *Filter*. Drop-down arrows appear next to each column heading.

Click the drop-down arrow next to the column heading you want to filter. The *Filter* menu will appear. Uncheck the boxes you don't want to view or click the box next to *Select All* to uncheck all boxes, and then check the boxes you do want to view. Click *OK*. All the other rows on the worksheet are now hidden.

Filtered row numbers appear in blue and the drop-down arrow changes to a filter symbol. You also see the number of records found in the status bar at the bottom of the screen .

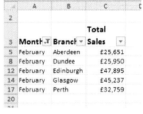

You can continue to refine your data by filtering on other columns.

To add another filter

Click the drop-down arrow beside the column heading where you would like to add another filter. For example within the month column we now want to find data for the Aberdeen branch.

Uncheck the boxes you don't want to view and check the box next to Aberdeen. Click *OK*.

To clear a filter

Click the drop-down arrow in the column and select *Clear Filter From*. The filter will be cleared from that column and you will now be able to see the data again.

To clear all filters

To clear all filters, simply click the *Filter* command on the *Data* tab.

Creating advanced filters

In a column of figures, such as total sales, you might want to find values within a certain range. Clicking on *Number Filters* will give you options. Selecting any of these options will open the *Custom AutoFilter* window where you can enter specific values.

Note that when specifying criteria you can also choose *And* or *Or*.

- The **And** function will return results that meet **both** criteria.
- The **Or** function will return results that meet **either** criterion.

Similarly, columns containing text or dates will offer *Text Filters* and *Date Filters*.

DON'T FORGET

To remove any filters click on *Filter* command on the *Data* tab.

VIDEO LINK

Watch the clip at www.brightredbooks.net for more on filtering data.

ONLINE

To learn about advanced filtering, head to www.brightredbooks.net

 THINGS TO DO AND THINK ABOUT

Head to www.brightredbooks.net to the folder called *Sorting and Filtering* for a number of exercises where you can practise your skills.

OUTLINING AND GROUPING DATA

HOW TO OUTLINE AND GROUP DATA

Outlining and **Grouping** data lets you organise data into groups and show or hide them from view. You can also summarise data for quick analysis using the **Subtotal** command.

Because outlining relies on grouping data that is related, you must sort before you can outline.

Example:
You want to find the subtotal for each month. The data has been sorted into chronological order. Click anywhere in the data then on **Subtotal**.

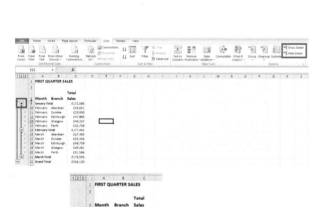

Line 1: *At each change in:* – use the drop-down arrow and choose how you want the data outlined. To find the subtotal for each month, select **Month** from the list.

Line 2: *Use function:* – use the drop-down arrow and choose from a list of functions. To add the total sales, choose **Sum**.

Line 3: *Add subtotal to:* – choose the column for the subtotal to appear in (here it is **Total Sales**).

Replace current subtotals means that if subtotals already exist in the worksheet they will be overwritten and ***Summary below data*** means a *Grand Total* will be included. These are ticked by default. Click **OK**.

The content of the worksheet is outlined, with each month placed in its own group and a subtotal calculated below each group.

Showing and hiding data

Click on the *Hide Detail* ⊟ or *Show Detail* ⊞ buttons. These are also available on the *Data* tab. Select a cell, then click the appropriate command.

To view groups by level

Based on their hierarchy, groups in the outline are placed in levels. You can display more or less information by clicking the level symbols 1 2 3 to the left of the worksheet.

Click the **highest level** to view and expand all of the groups.
Click the **next level** to hide the detail of the previous level.
Click the **lowest level** to display the lowest level of detail.

Removing groups and subtotalling

Select the rows or columns you want to ungroup then click *Ungroup* on the *Data* tab.

To ungroup all groups, open the drop-down menu *Ungroup* and choose *Clear Outline*.

Ungroup and *Clear Outline* will not remove subtotalling: this stays in place and continues to function until you remove it.

To ungroup data and remove subtotalling click the *Subtotal* command then click *Remove All*.

WORKING WITH MULTIPLE WORKSHEETS

To organise a workbook and make it easier to navigate, worksheet tabs can be renamed and colour-coded. New worksheets can also be inserted, deleted, moved and copied.

To rename a **worksheet tab** right-click on it and select **Rename**. Key in the name you want to give your worksheet. Click anywhere outside the tab and the worksheet is renamed. Similarly choose **Tab Color** from the **worksheet menu** and then select a colour.

Delete and **Move or Copy...** are also available on the **worksheet menu**. It is quicker, however, to click on the worksheet you want to move – the mouse will then change to show a small worksheet icon. Now drag the worksheet icon to the new position which will be indicated by a small black arrow. Release the mouse and the worksheet moves.

To copy a worksheet hold down the **Ctrl** key and at the same time click on the tab of the worksheet. A small worksheet icon with a cross in the middle appears . Drag this to the new position and release the mouse and the **Ctrl** key. Notice that the new worksheet will have the same name but with (2) after it.

To insert a new worksheet click on the **Insert Worksheet** icon.

Grouping and ungrouping worksheets

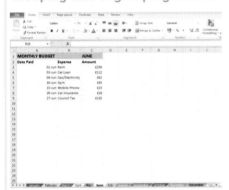

You can work with each worksheet individually or in a group. This means that any changes made to one worksheet in a group will be made to every worksheet in the group.

For example, imagine you have set up a budget sheet for each month showing all your expenses. At the start of June you decide to cancel your gym membership. By **grouping** the worksheets from June to December you can simply make the change to the first worksheet in the group and all other worksheets will be updated at the same time.

To group worksheets, select the first worksheet then press and hold the **Ctrl** key on your keyboard and use the mouse to select each of the remaining worksheets you want in the group. Release the **Ctrl** key. The worksheet tabs appear white for grouped worksheets and at the top of the screen you will see the word **[Group]** after the file name.

You can work in any of the group worksheets and make changes that will appear on every worksheet in that group. But be careful – if you click a worksheet tab that is not in the group all of your worksheets will become ungrouped. You can also ungroup by right-clicking one of the worksheet tabs and selecting **Ungroup Sheets**.

 ## THINGS TO DO AND THINK ABOUT

Head to www.brightredbooks.net to the folder called *Outlining and Grouping Data* for a number of exercises where you can practise your skills.

DON'T FORGET

If the tab colour still appears to be white it is because the worksheet is still selected. Select any other worksheet to see the colour change.

DON'T FORGET

To quickly select adjacent worksheets click on the first worksheet tab in the group, press and hold down the **Shift** key and then click the worksheet tab of the last worksheet in the group.

DON'T FORGET

Adding colour to worksheet tabs can help identify which are included in any grouping as all the tabs of worksheets within a group will change to white.

VIDEO LINK

Learn more about outlining at www.brightredbooks.net

ONLINE TEST

Test yourself on this topic online at www.brightredbooks.net

LINKING CELL REFERENCES AND CREATING CHARTS

LINKING CELLS BETWEEN WORKSHEETS AND 3D REFERENCES

You can use data from one worksheet cell in calculations in another worksheet by creating a link between the cells. Linked data immediately reflects any changes made to the original data.

For example, imagine you keep a record of all your monthly household expenditure and income in a workbook file. Any money left over at the end of one month is added to what is available to spend the following month. To link the worksheets and enter the amount automatically, carry out the following four steps:

Step 1: Click on the cell where you want the data to go.

Step 2: Key in the = sign.

Step 3: Click the worksheet and the cell you want to retrieve the information from (January/C21).

Step 4: Press **Enter**. The information is now copied over.

Look at the formula bar and you will see that the completed formula is =**January!C21**. This means that the source of the cell is the January worksheet. Should the January figure change, the February figure will automatically update. All months can be linked in this way – February to March and so on.

3D cell references

A 3D reference is a reference that refers to the same cell or range of cells on multiple worksheets. Using a 3D reference is a useful way to consolidate data from several worksheets that follow the same pattern and that contain the same type of data.

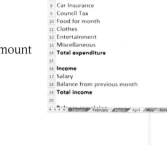

For example, imagine that at the end of the year you want to total your monthly expenditure for all the different expense items. The steps required are quite tricky and must be followed in this order:

Step 1: Click on the cell where you want the answer to appear. Click on **AutoSum** ∑ or key in =SUM(

Step 2: Click on the first worksheet to be included in the group (January) then hold down **Shift** and click on the last worksheet (December).

Step 3: Click on the relevant cell in the first worksheet – the amount paid for rent in January.

Step 4: Key in) to signify the end of the formula.

Step 5: Press **Enter**.

The formula will read =**SUM(January:December!C3)**.

This means that the computer will go through every worksheet in the range and add together all rent that has been paid during the year.

DON'T FORGET

To select sequential worksheets, click the first worksheet you wish to include in the 3D reference then hold the **Shift** key and click the last worksheet you wish to include. To select non-sequential worksheets hold the **Ctrl** key and click on each of the worksheets you wish to include in the 3D reference.

DON'T FORGET

There is a limit to the type of calculations that can make up a 3D reference. The following functions can be used: SUM, AVERAGE, COUNT, COUNTA, MAX and MIN.

DON'T FORGET

Moving, copying, inserting or deleting worksheets included in a 3D reference may result in data in the specified cells being included or deleted – check carefully to ensure you have included all the worksheets you want to include.

CHARTING

Charts show the meaning behind numbers and clearly display comparisons and trends. Various types of charts are available from the **Charts** group; choose one that effectively represents your data.

contd

The ones most frequently used are:

- **Column charts** – vertical bars represent data (often used for comparing information)

- **Line charts** – data points are connected with lines (ideal for showing trends)

- **Pie charts** – each value is shown as a slice of the pie (good for comparing proportions)

- **Bar charts** – just like **column charts** but using horizontal instead of vertical bars

Creating a chart

To create a chart select the information to be included and click on the type of chart you want.

Once the chart has been created more options become available in **Chart Tools**.

Chart Tools – Design tab

The commands you are most likely to use on the **Design** tab under **Chart Tools** are:

Switch Row/Column – Excel plots data according to the number of rows and columns in the chart – the larger number is placed on the horizontal axis. When there are equal rows and columns, rows go on the vertical axis and columns on the horizontal axis. To change the way the data is presented go to **Chart Tools Design** and click on **Switch Row/Column**.

Select Data – if you have not selected the column headings, the **Legend** refers to series of data. To change this, choose **Select Data** and within the **Legend Entries (Series)** box, click on **Series 1** then **Edit**. You can either key in the name or click on the appropriate cell in the worksheet. Click **OK**.

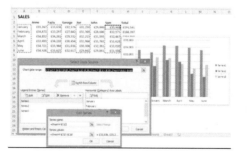

Move Chart – charts are created within the same worksheet as the data being plotted. To move the chart to a new worksheet, click **Move Chart** and name the new worksheet to contain the chart.

THINGS TO DO AND THINK ABOUT

Head to www.brightredbooks.net to the folder called *Linking Cell References* for a number of exercises where you can practise your skills.

DON'T FORGET

To create a chart using data from different parts of the worksheet, select the first column then hold down the *Ctrl* key and select the remaining data. For example, imagine you want to plot sales for Fazia, Joe and Sam for January to June only – these columns are shaded blue.

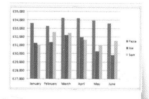

DON'T FORGET

Including the column headings in your selection automatically creates a *Legend*.

DON'T FORGET

All these commands have drop-down menus which give you further choices or will open appropriate dialog boxes.

VIDEO LINK

Watch the clip at www.brightredbooks.net to learn more about 3D references.

CHARTS AND PIVOT TABLES

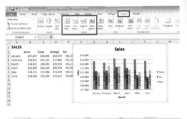

CHARTS

Chart Tools – Layout tab

These commands have drop-down menus for further choices or open appropriate dialog boxes:

Chart Title – give charts appropriate titles.

Axis Titles – give the horizontal and the vertical axes meaningful titles.

Legend – provide a legend when different colours are used to display sets of data.

Data Labels – place labels outside or within bars, rotate and show values, percentages or names.

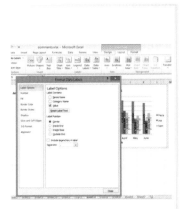

PIVOT TABLES

Pivot tables (or **Pivot table reports**) make the data in your worksheet more manageable by summarising it and allowing you to manipulate it in different ways. A pivot table is composed of rows, columns and data. Before constructing a pivot table, try to visualise the general layout of the pivot table based on the question you are trying to answer.

For example, in this worksheet you have been asked to find total sales by branch and by month. The information should be presented with branch and month being either the row or column. Total sales means the data should be summed.

Therefore, this pivot table will be structured as follows:

- **Branch** will occupy the **row** fields position in the pivot table.
- **Month** will occupy the **column** fields position in the pivot table.
- **Total sales** will occupy the **value** fields position in the pivot table.

Creating a pivot table

First, ensure the range has column headings and that there are no blank rows.

Place your cursor anywhere in the data apart from in the headings, click *Insert* and then *PivotTable*.

Under *Choose the data that you want to analyse*, you can replace the automatic range with one of your choice.

Under *Choose where you want the PivotTable report to be placed*, choose *New Worksheet*. Then click *OK*.

A new worksheet opens with a **Blank Pivot Table** on the left and the *Field List* on the right.

Now drag the fields you want from the *PivotTable Field List* into the relevant area below. Earlier it was decided that **Branch** should go to *Row Labels*, **Month** should go to *Column Labels* and **Total Sales** will go to Σ *Values* where it will be analysed.

ONLINE

Learn about printing charts at www.brightredbooks.net

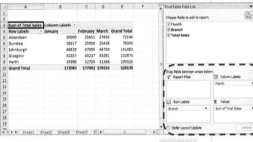

contd

As the fields are dragged into the relevant areas you will see the pivot table being constructed and a tick will appear next to the field name.

When the **Total Sales** field is dragged to the Σ *Values* area, the pivot table will automatically give a grand total for each **Branch** and for each **Month** as well as an overall grand total.

To change the way the data is summarised click on the drop-down arrow at *Sum of Total Sales* and choose the type of calculation you want.

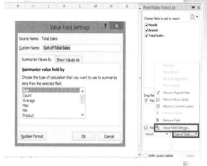

Changing the layout of a pivot table

Swap the field names between *Column* and *Row*, 'pivoting' the data. Remember that a calculation will be carried out on any field put into Σ *Values*.

As with a normal spreadsheet, data in a pivot table can be sorted using the *Sort* command on the *Data* tab. You can also apply any type of formatting you want; for example, you can change the number format to currency.

Pivot tables don't update automatically. To manually update, select the pivot table and click *Refresh*.

DON'T FORGET

Labels should be edited to make them more meaningful – for example, this one should read **Branch**.

Pivot table filters

Filters on column and row headings display data for specific items and filter out everything else.

Sum of Total Sales	Column Labels			
Row Labels	January	February	March	Grand Total
Aberdeen	20000	25651	27493	73144
Grand Total	20000	25651	27493	73144

In addition, the pivot table *Report Filter* allows you to create a pivot table and then use one or more fields as filters on the pivot table. This will allow you to focus on a portion of the data and filter out everything else.

Drag a field from the *Field List* into the *Report Filter* area. In this example, it is the **Branch** field.

The field that is being used as a filter now appears above the pivot table.

Click the drop-down arrow on the field to view the list of items. Select the item you want to filter on or click on *Select Multiple Items* to filter on any number of items – in this example, it is Aberdeen and Glasgow.

Clicking the drop-down arrow at the filter icon will allow you to change the filter – for example, to filter only on Edinburgh.

VIDEO LINK

Head to www.brightredbooks.net and check out the clip about pivot tables.

THINGS TO DO AND THINK ABOUT

Head to www.brightredbooks.net to the folders called *Charting* and *Pivot Tables* for a number of exercises where you can practise your skills.

PIVOT CHARTS, COMMENTS AND WORKING BETWEEN APPLICATIONS

VIDEO LINK

Head to www.brightredbooks.net and check out the clips for more on this topic.

PIVOT CHARTS

Pivot charts display data from a pivot table. As with regular charts, you choose the chart type, layout and style to best represent the data. Here, we use a pivot chart to show trends by branch.

To create a pivot chart

Select any cell in the pivot table and the *Options* tab will appear. Click the *PivotChart* command.

From the *Insert Chart* dialog box, select the desired chart type, for example Column, then click *OK*.

The pivot chart will appear in the worksheet along with the *PivotChart Tools* contextual tab which allows you to move the chart to a new worksheet, add a title/axis labels and so on.

As with a pivot table, it is possible to swap the column headings and change the way the data is analysed, and the drop-down arrows allow filters to be applied.

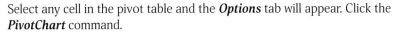

DON'T FORGET

If you make any changes to the pivot table, the pivot chart will adjust automatically.

USING COMMENTS IN A SPREADSHEET

Adding notes to a worksheet in the form of **comments** helps you make a worksheet easier to understand by providing additional context for the data. You can use a comment as a note that provides information about data in an individual cell. You can also add a comment to a column heading to provide guidance on data that a user should enter.

When a cell has a comment, a red indicator appears in the top right corner of the cell and when you rest the pointer on the cell, the comment appears.

Comments can be added, edited and formatted, moved, resized, copied, displayed or hidden. You can control how they and their indicators are displayed and you can delete comments after use.

Add a comment

Click on *New Comment* on the *Review* tab. (If a comment already exists in the cell, *New Comment* will change to *Edit Comment*.)

The comment is created and a marker appears in the cell. By default, the new comment is labelled with a name (which might be your computer user name), but this can be edited or deleted.

contd

You can now type the comment text within the comment box. When you click outside the comment box, the comment box disappears but the comment indicator remains. To keep the comment visible click **Show/Hide Comment** in the **Comments** group on the **Review** tab.

Within the **Comments** group on the **Review** tab are the command buttons to **Edit** or **Delete** a comment and to move backwards and forwards between the comments.

By default, text in comments uses the Tahoma font in size 8. You cannot change the default font that is used, but you can change the format of the comment text in each comment by right-clicking the comment text, and then clicking **Format Comment**.

Move or resize a comment

Right-click the cell that has the comment that you want to change, and then click **Show/ Hide Comments**. Click the comment box border so that sizing handles appear. Make sure that the pointer is not in the comment.

Do one of the following:

- To move the comment, drag the border of the comment box, or press an arrow key.

- To resize the comment, drag the handles on the sides and corners of the comment box.

Copy comments to other cells

Select the cell or cells that contain the comments and select **Copy**. Click on the cell where you want to paste the comment and then click on the drop-down arrow below **Paste** and select **Paste Special**. The **Paste Special** dialog box will open. Under **Paste** click on the radio button beside **Comments** then click **OK** and the comment will be copied.

WORKING BETWEEN APPLICATIONS

Copying from Access into Excel

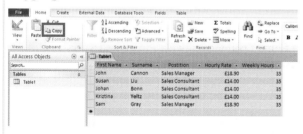

Open the table, query or form that has been saved in Access and that contains the records that you want to copy. In **Datasheet View** select the records you want to copy and then click on the **Copy** command on the **Home** tab. Open the spreadsheet file that you want to copy to and click in the upper-left corner of the worksheet area where you want the first field name to appear. On the **Home** tab, in the **Clipboard** group, click **Paste**. Check the formatting, font and so on to ensure consistency.

THINGS TO DO AND THINK ABOUT

Head to www.brightredbooks.net to the folders called *Pivot Charts* and *Using Comments* for a number of exercises where you can practise your skills.

DON'T FORGET

A very quick way of adding a comment to a cell is to press the **Shift** key **+ F2** key.

DON'T FORGET

You can also right-click the cell that contains the comment, and then click **Show/Hide Comments**.

DON'T FORGET

When you sort data in a worksheet, comments are sorted together with the data. However, in pivot table reports, comments do not move with the cell when you change the layout of the report.

DON'T FORGET

Do not press **Enter** after you click **OK**. If you do, the cell contents will be copied to the paste area in addition to the comment.

DON'T FORGET

Copied comments replace any existing comments in the destination area.

DON'T FORGET

To ensure that the copied records do not replace existing records, make sure that the worksheet has no data below or to the right of the cell that you click.

WORKING BETWEEN APPLICATIONS AND PRINTING

WORKING BETWEEN APPLICATIONS

Connect Access data to Excel

Connecting Access data to Excel means you can automatically refresh your workbook from the Access database whenever it is updated with new information.

Click the cell where you want to insert the data from the Access database. On the **Data** tab, in the **Get External Data** group, click **From Access**. The **Select Data Source** window opens. Find the Access database that you want to import. Click **Open** and then click the table or query to be imported and click **OK**.

Import Data allows you to choose a **Table** or a **Pivot Table Report/Chart** as well as whether to use the **Existing worksheet** or a **New worksheet**.

To update your worksheet with changes from the database, click **Refresh** on the **Data** tab.

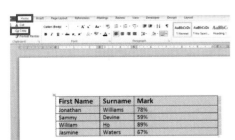

Copying a table from Word into Excel

After pasting a Word table into an Excel worksheet, you may have to clean it up so that you can use Excel's calculation features.

Select the entire table or the rows and columns that you want to copy to an Excel worksheet. On the **Home** tab click on **Copy**.

In the Excel worksheet, select the upper-left corner of the worksheet area and click **Paste**. Using the drop-down menu below **Paste**, you can choose to **Keep Source Formatting** (the table gridlines will be copied) or **Match Destination Formatting** (there will be no gridlines).

Copying a chart to a Word document

VIDEO LINK

Watch the clips at www.brightredbooks.net to learn more about spreadsheets.

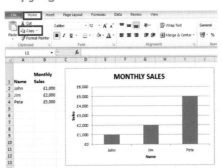

In the spreadsheet, select the chart to be copied, making sure you select the whole chart and not just the plot area, and click **Copy**.

In the Word document, click where you want to paste the copied chart. Click on the drop-down arrow below **Paste** and select **Paste Special**. In the **As** box ensure **Microsoft Excel Chart Object** is selected.

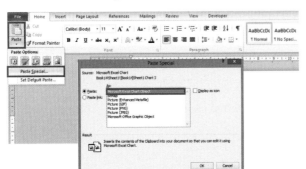

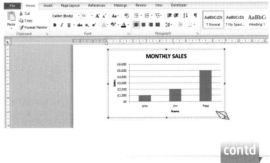

contd

If necessary, resize the graph diagonally to keep it in proportion. If the text becomes too small, double-click on the chart area, select each area of text and then change the font size and so on. Notice that when you double-click, the **Chart Tools** tab opens which allows you to make other changes to **Design**, **Layout** and **Format** just as you would be able to do in the spreadsheet file.

If the chart is based on data that is likely to change and you want the chart to reflect the latest information, click **Paste Link**. Right-click on the chart and select **Update Link** to show any changes made to the spreadsheet in the Word document.

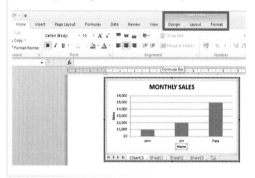

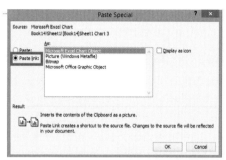

PRINTING

Excel spreadsheets are designed to be as long and as wide as you need. This is great for editing and viewing on screen but can make them difficult to fit to a standard sheet of paper. This does not mean, however, that it is impossible to make a worksheet look good on paper.

Preview your worksheet before you print

Click **Print** to see exactly how your worksheet will look on the printed page. The button at the bottom right-hand corner lets you see the margins which you can then drag and modify if necessary.

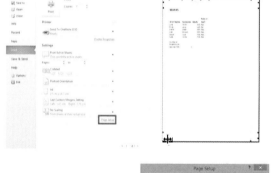

There are various options available in this window, but even more options are available in **Page Setup**.

Here are a number of tabs which can be selected and where changes can be made. For example, on the **Page** tab, the orientation can be changed and **Fit to 1 page** can be selected.

Printing choices are also available from **Page Setup**, **Scale to Fit** and **Sheet Options** on the **Page Layout** tab. For example, **Print Area** lets you print a range of cells rather than the full worksheet

In any assessment task you will always be asked to print your worksheet in **Formula View** to prove that you have used formulae and not just keyed in the answer (go to the **Formulas** tab then select **Show Formulas**). Always ensure that the complete formula can be seen and that it is not truncated, otherwise you will not be credited with the marks. **Formula View** is normally printed with row and column headings and gridlines, as this makes it easier to check formulae.

THE EFFECTIVENESS OF ADMINISTRATIVE PRACTICES WITHIN ORGANISATIONS

WHAT IS AN ADMINISTRATIVE ASSISTANT?

An Administrative Assistant is an individual who provides various kinds of administrative support to people and groups in business enterprises.

Work undertaken by an Administrative Assistant

The Administrative Assistant is likely to be involved in the planning and organising of events, such as business meetings and conferences. As such they will be expected to be able to multi-task and undertake a broad range of duties including:

- filing information and documents (manually and using computerised databases) and being able to find them again when necessary. They must also ensure confidentiality of private and sensitive information.
- recording information in e-diaries and organising meeting and events. They would also organise travel and accommodation for staff on business trips.
- creating and updating databases and spreadsheets which ensures efficient information handling.
- preparing a range of business documents including letters, agendas, invoices and reports to a professional standard using appropriate computer software.
- dealing with requests for information (electronic/paper and verbal) from colleagues or customers.
- reprographic tasks including photocopying documents and booklets, and binding and scanning documents.
- overseeing the maintenance of non-computing office equipment to ensure it is in good working order (for example, copiers, printers, collators and laminators).
- ensuring office supplies are replenished as and when necessary (for example paper, office stationery, printer toner).
- operating a petty cash system to reimburse staff if they have used their own money to pay for business items, for example taxi fares.
- reception duties including greeting and looking after visitors, answering the telephone and making appointments.

DON'T FORGET

One of the main roles of an administrative assistant is to plan and organise events such as business meetings and conferences.

DON'T FORGET

A quality is part of your personality. A skill is something you can learn or develop.

ONLINE

There are great activities for this topic at www.brightredbooks.net

ONLINE TEST

Head to www.brightredbooks.net to test your knowledge of this topic.

QUALITIES AND SKILLS OF AN ADMINISTRATIVE ASSISTANT

A highly effective Administrative Assistant should possess the following qualities and skills:

QUALITIES	SKILLS
Hard-working	Effective communicator
Enthusiastic	Computer literacy and IT
Reliable and dependable	Problem-solving
Honest and trustworthy	Teamwork
Flexible and willing to learn	Planning and organising
Accurate and careful	
Polite	
Able to get on well with others	
Able to cope with pressure	
Tolerant of others	

TIME AND TASK MANAGEMENT

Time management is a very important skill for all employees. Many employees find themselves frustrated with their workload and this often leads to stress as they try to catch up on tasks that they have not managed to complete.

Skills required for effective time and task management

- **Planning** – Employees must plan the use of their time and resources. There are many tools available to help with this, from simple daily to-do lists to more long-term action plans or development plans. (These will be explained in more detail later.)
- **Prioritising** – Employees must be able to decide which tasks are most important and should be carried out first and which ones are less important and so can be completed later in the day or week.
- **Organisation** – Employees should look ahead to identify future tasks that will be required to be undertaken.
- **Assertiveness** – Employees must be able to say 'no' when it is clear that they have taken on too much work.
- **Negotiation** – Employees must show confidence and be able to negotiate revised deadlines and request additional resources when necessary.
- **Control** – Employees must exercise control by keeping calm and tackling tasks in order of priority.
- **Evaluation** – Employees should review and evaluate all work undertaken, identify the causes of any problems and implement strategies that will lead to improvement.
- **Resource management** – Employees must ensure efficient use of all resources including staff, time and equipment.
- **Directing** – Some employees will be required to direct other employees to get the work done. This will involve leadership, communication, motivation and delegation.

Effective time and task management will bring benefits to both the individual and the organisation. Poor time and task management, on the other hand, will have a negative impact on both the individual employee and the organisation.

EFFECTS OF POOR TIME/TASK MANAGEMENT	BENEFITS OF GOOD TIME/TASK MANAGEMENT
Staff may become stressed and this can in turn lead to absences from work	Lower stress levels which will reduce staff absences
A decrease in morale and job satisfaction, leading to high rates of absenteeism and staff turnover, which in turn causes increased recruitment and training costs	Improved morale and job satisfaction for employees, leading to a reduction in staff absenteeism and staff turnover, which in turn reduces recruitment and training costs
Reduction in productivity as work is not produced efficiently or to the correct standard	Increased productivity and an improvement in the quality of work produced
Poor working relationships with colleagues and management	Improved working relationships with colleagues and management
Poor customer relations and increase in customer complaints	Good customer relations as targets and deadlines are likely to be met

 THINGS TO DO AND THINK ABOUT

A vacancy has arisen in your school office for the post of Administrative Assistant. You are required to produce an advert for the post to be sent to the local job centre.

Instructions
- Visit the school office and speak with the Office Manager. You should find out as much information as you can about working in the school office as an Administrative Assistant. You can also make use of the internet to view vacancies for Administrative Assistant posts. Once you have gathered all the information you need you should use word processing software to create an advertisement for the job vacancy.
- Your advertisement should include the following information:
  - Skills and qualities required for the post
  - Duties to be undertaken
  - Type of contract and conditions of employment (hours and holidays etc.)
  - Annual salary
  - Any other relevant information you have gathered from your research
  - Print one copy of your advertisement.

TIME AND TASK MANAGEMENT

TIME STEALERS

TIME STEALER	SOLUTION
Interruption from telephone and visitors	Learn to politely control the conversation and suggest meeting at another appropriate time.
Taking on too much work	Be assertive and learn to say 'no'. Discuss your workload with your line manager and look for opportunities to delegate tasks to subordinates.
Desk stress	Avoid a cluttered and untidy desk. Make use of desk filing trays and operate a clear desk policy to ensure all documents can be located quickly.
Meetings that take longer than necessary	Ensure that meetings have time limits and think about making use of timers or alarms so that those present at the meeting know how much time they have to talk. Ensure that agendas are realistic.
Making unnecessary journeys	Group jobs together so that visits to the photocopier or other departments are carried out only once or twice per day.
Procrastination	Use a to-do list or a priorities list and ensure that one task is fully completed before another task is started.
Unclear or poor communication	There should be a clear line of communication between subordinate and line manager. Clarification should be sought when there is any uncertainty about a task.
Crisis management	Avoid reacting hastily to an emergency or unexpected situation. Take time to plan a realistic and achievable solution.
Lack of forward planning	Make use of planning aids such as priority lists and action plans.

DELEGATION

Delegation is where responsibility and/or authority is given to another person (usually from a manager to a subordinate) to carry out certain activities/tasks.

Delegation is also very important for time and task management, not only because it helps to develop staff and improve motivation, but because it also saves time and leaves the manager free to get on with more important tasks.

Unfortunately, some managers find delegation very difficult because:

- they think they can always do the job better themselves
- their standards are too high
- they are afraid of losing control.

A manager who fails to delegate will:

- suffer from stress as a result of trying to manage a heavy workload, which could lead to illness and absenteeism
- often miss deadlines for tasks and their work may not be of the highest standard
- fail to develop staff, which means that no-one will be able to stand in as deputy if the manager is absent
- cause their team to suffer from low morale and job satisfaction, which could result in the manager having to spend more time counselling staff and organising team-building activities
- spend more time recruiting and training new staff as existing employees leave to seek professional development and progression with another organisation
- miss out on promotional opportunities.

VIDEO LINK

Go online and watch the video at www.brightredbooks.net

DON'T FORGET

Time stealers are time-wasting activities that 'steal' time from an employee and reduce their effectiveness in the workplace. Some of the more common time stealers and suggestions for dealing with them are outlined above.

VIDEO LINK

Check out the clip at www.brightredbooks.net

DON'T FORGET

Delegation is where a manager gives responsibility and authority to a subordinate for completion of a task.

ONLINE TEST

Try out the activities at www.brightredbooks.net for more on this topic.

CASE STUDY

Consequences of bad time and task management

Stephen Duncan is a Project Manager at a voluntary organisation in Edinburgh. He has provided you with the following information regarding his job.

'My job feels really overwhelming. I'm managing three major projects simultaneously, each of which could alone easily fill the timescale I have for doing all of them. Because I'm managing a team of volunteers to push these projects forward as fast as possible, there are constant interruptions – visitors, e-mails and telephone calls. Other high organisational priorities constantly come up and require hours of effort. I feel like I can't get anything done, timelines are slipping, the quality of the work isn't as good as I'd like and I constantly feel behind.

'The small organisation that I work for is very well run and I have an incredible boss. So it really does feel like it's my fault things aren't going well. To be honest, I don't figure out what I need fast enough, I don't say "that deadline is unrealistic", I don't inform my manger that "if we expand Project Number 1, the deadline for Project Number 2 will slip by months". If I could say all these things, people probably would offer to help.

'I am a bit of a perfectionist and sometimes feel that business reports and correspondence to clients will be more professional if I do them myself, and this is adding to the demands on my time.

'I really want to be good at this job, and for those brief stretches when things are under control, it's exciting and fun and I experience job satisfaction. However, there are occasions when I become completely burned out – discouraged, apathetic, hopeless and unhappy. I simply end up moving from one job to another, juggling tasks and achieving nothing!'

Questions

1   Stephen's work is being affected by poor time and task management. Outline a consequence of this for Stephen and a consequence for the organisation he works for.

2   Identify from the passage four time stealers that are affecting Stephen's work and suggest a strategy that could be used to address each one of these.

3   Give one reason why Stephen is reluctant to delegate tasks to other employees.

4   Describe two consequences of Stephen's reluctance to delegate work to others.

THINGS TO DO AND THINK ABOUT

1   Outline any two skills and any two qualities which an Administrative Assistant should possess.

2   Briefly describe some of the tasks that an Administrative Assistant would be expected to undertake.

3   Describe any two consequences of poor time and task management.

4   Suggest strategies that an Administrative Assistant could employ to ensure effective time and task management.

5   Describe the consequences for an employee who does not take the opportunity to delegate.

 ONLINE TEST

Head to www.brightredbooks.net to test yourself on time and task management.

SETTING TARGETS FOR THE INDIVIDUAL AND THE ORGANISATION 1

It is very important within any organisation that staff share the management's vision. One of the duties of the Senior Administrative Assistant is to set both personal and departmental **targets** to enable the organisation to meet its long-term aims and objectives. Departmental targets will only be achieved by employees working as a team and working towards achieving their own personal objectives.

WHY SET TARGETS?

There are a number of reasons why targets should be set for both individual employees and the organisation as a whole. Setting targets helps

- measure the success of an organisation
- managers organise their resources (both financial and human)
- all employees to understand what the organisation wishes to achieve
- all employees to understand their role in the organisation
- employees to measure the success of their work compared with the original targets set

Example: Targets

Here are some examples of targets a company might set:
- Reduce customer complaints by 20 per cent.
- Increase keyboarding speed from 50 words per minute to 75 words per minute.
- Increase sales by 20 per cent per quarter.
- Maintain a clear and tidy workstation.
- Reduce time taken to file documents.
- Reduce unnecessary photocopying to try to reduce administrative costs.

'SMART' TARGETS

It is not enough to simply set targets – targets need to be SMART!

S	**Specific** – The target must be well defined and state exactly what is required or is to be achieved.
M	**Measurable** – It must be quantifiable and be expressed in some form of measurement unit, for example, increase sales by 20 per cent.
A	**Agreed** – The target must be discussed and agreed with your line manager, especially when preparing your personal development plan (PDP).
R	**Realistic** – Targets should be challenging but must still be achievable.
T	**Timed** – It is important that key dates identify when the target should be completed.

DON'T FORGET

A number of planning aids can be used to record and monitor targets.

PLANNING AIDS

Target setting (both at individual and organisational level) will be based on a number of factors and should be recorded and monitored using a variety of different documents such as those shown in the table below.

NAME OF DOCUMENT	DESCRIPTION
Gantt chart	This is used by project managers to show comparisons between work planned and work accomplished in relation to time schedules. It looks a bit like a bar chart.
To-do list	Usually a note to yourself to show a list of tasks that need to be completed. These may be pre-printed to-do lists or simple sticky notes or sheets of scrap paper.
Priorities list	Similar to a to-do list but this time put in order of priority showing which task needs to be tackled first, which second and so on.
Action plan	A document that identifies what should be done by whom, with expected completion dates.
Electronic diary (e-diary)	Useful for arranging meetings as days, weeks and months can be seen at a glance, and the e-diaries of all participants can be seen at the same time. Most e-diaries have electronic task lists which aid planning and organisation.
Personal development plan	A formal document that allows an employee to record areas of strength and areas where training and development are required. This helps the employee to meet targets set. Some organisations also encourage employees to record personal aims. Although not a requirement of the job, these may enhance the employee's confidence and well-being.

contd

Let's now look at an example of each.

Gantt chart

This is a chart that allows individuals to see at a glance key dates and tasks and to monitor when tasks have been completed. The Gantt chart below plots the time plan horizontally and the tasks to be completed vertically.

Example:

This Gantt chart shows the planning and organising of a jobs fair over a 13-week period.

ACTIVITY/WEEK	1	2	3	4	5	6	7	8	9	10	11	12	13
Create database of local businesses, colleges and training agencies													
Research and book a suitable venue for the jobs fair conference													
Prepare an itinerary for the one-day event													
Send letters of invitation to potential delegates													
Prepare publicity materials and distribute													
Update database with delegate responses and their requirements													
Plan layout of room and produce guides for job-seekers													
Source potential caterers and budget for catering costs													
Prepare evaluation forms for both delegates and job-seekers													
Update database from information on evaluation forms													

Priorities lists

A priorities list is very similar to a to-do list. In this type of list, however, tasks to be completed are prioritised so that more urgent tasks are undertaken first. Employees usually also estimate how much time each task will take to complete and this helps ensure that as many tasks as possible on the list can be carried out.

PRIORITY	TASK	TIME	CHANGES OR PROBLEMS	COMPLETED/CARRIED FORWARD
1	Check and distribute incoming mail including e-mails	30 mins		✓
4	Type up notice of meeting and agenda for next month's managers' meeting	20 mins		✓
5	E-mail notice of meeting and agenda to all department managers and directors	10 mins	Check agenda items for other paperwork	Started – network problems. Carried forward
2	Meet with departmental manager to discuss today's tasks	30 mins	Manager unexpectedly absent	Not started
3	Type up minutes of last department managers' meeting	30 mins		✓

THINGS TO DO AND THINK ABOUT

You are an Administrative Assistant at Campbell and Clark Ltd.

Simon Gregg, the Human Resources Manager, wishes to highlight to all staff the impact that time stealers can have on their workflow and suggest possible measures that staff can take to avoid them.

He has asked that you prepare a short PowerPoint presentation outlining six time stealers and strategies that staff can use to address them. Make your presentation as informative as possible and forward to Mr Gregg for approval.

SETTING TARGETS FOR THE INDIVIDUAL AND THE ORGANISATION 2

PLANNING AIDS

Action plan

Producing an action plan can be beneficial not only for individual employees but also for the company as a whole. For example, it allows project managers or any member of the company to monitor progress and look at each task step by step, therefore allowing the efficient handling and ultimate success of the project. The advantages of creating action plans are that they allow you to execute a structured plan for the end goal you intend to achieve and they provide the team with appropriate foundations, therefore allowing them to prioritise the amount of time they spend on each task. This will then prevent any sidetracking that may occur.

ACTION REQUIRED/TASKS TO BE COMPLETED	ESTIMATED TIME FOR COMPLETION	ACTUAL TIME TAKEN TO COMPLETE	NOTES
Discuss with Sales Manager and sales representatives information required from market research	2 hours	3 hours	Compile a list of information required by sales staff
Prepare a survey to undertake market research	3 hours	5 hours	
Meet and train market research personnel on procedures for carrying out market research	2 days	1·5 days	Monitor market research staff to ensure all procedures are being followed
Carry out market research	4 days	3 days	Many members of the public volunteered to take part in survey and so three days was sufficient to gather required data
Prepare a presentation/report for sales staff outlining main findings from market research	3 hours	4 hours	Allow time for questions and discussion during the presentation

To-do list

This is a document that can be used on a day-to-day basis to remind the individual of the tasks that need to be completed. Pre-printed forms and pads are available but many staff simply create their own to-do lists in a notepad. A to-do list should be completed at the end of each working day for tasks to be undertaken the next day.

PERSONAL DEVELOPMENT PLAN

This is a specially designed form that allows employees to formally record areas of their job where they are demonstrating key strengths and areas of their job where they require support and/or further development through training. Employees normally prepare a personal development plan annually and should discuss the plan with their line manager on a regular basis throughout the year. Preparing a personal development plan annually allows an employee to focus on key aspects of their job and identify skills they possess that could be shared with other employees in the organisation. More importantly, it allows them to identify training requirements which would allow them to improve their overall effectiveness within the organisation. A personal development plan is a 'working document' and can be updated/added to throughout the year. An example of a personal development plan is shown on the next page.

contd

Example:

Name of Employee: Helen Hamilton (Administrative Assistant)

DATE	KEY STRENGTHS IDENTIFIED	AREAS FOR DEVELOPMENT IDENTIFIED	DEVELOPMENT/TRAINING REQUIRED	TARGET DATE	NOTES FROM REVIEW MEETINGS	INITIALS
10 March	Creating spreadsheets using simple formulae. Using spreadsheets to produce graphs to present business information	Using named cells and making use of more complex formulae including absolute and conditional formulae	Attend training course at local Further Education college	20 November	Attended training course one night a week for 15 weeks. Now using new acquired skills in the workplace	HH ML
10 March	Entering, updating and deleting entries in an e-diary	Setting reminders and making use of electronic task lists	Training from senior receptionist	20 November	Senior receptionist acted as a mentor and provided coaching on using features of an e-diary	HH ML
20 April	Competent in all aspects of word processing software	Develop an understanding of and the necessary skills in PowerPoint presentation software	In-house training – attending company open learning unit to complete PowerPoint modules 1–3	15 December	To date has complete modules 1 and 2. Module 3 is in progress	HH ML
12 May	Excellent file management skills	Time and task management	Implement a range of measures/ strategies to reduce time stealers	15 December	A range of planning aids in place to ensure focus on key tasks	HH ML

Employee's signature: **Helen Hamilton**   Line manager's signature: **Mandy Low**

ELECTRONIC DIARY

An e-diary is a useful tool for an Administrative Assistant when arranging meetings, as days, weeks and months can be seen at a glance and the e-diaries of all participants can be seen and updated at the same time. The main features of an e-diary are as follows:

Automatic invitations	An e-diary can be used to send automatic invitations to meetings to all team members via e-mail. If the Administrative Assistant regularly checks their e-mail they should receive an instant decline or acceptance in response to invitations sent.
Recurring meetings	A series of meetings can be entered once and automatically filled into other dates for future meetings.
Reminders	Reminders of the date of a meeting can be set and this should ensure that no-one misses a meeting.
To-do lists	Tasks to be undertaken by an Administrative Assistant prior to a meeting can be listed and prioritised.
Double booking	An e-diary will alert the user to any appointments that when entered would result in a double booking.
Alarm facility	The Administrative Assistant can set alarms on the e-diary to remind them that a meeting is pending.

An e-diary with these features will assist an Administrative Assistant with both time and task management.

THINGS TO DO AND THINK ABOUT

You are Administrative Assistant at Taylor and Quinn PLC. You have a number of tasks to complete tomorrow. You start work at 8:00am and finish work at 4:00pm. You have one hour for lunch and a 20-minute break at 11:00am. The tasks that you are required to complete are as follows:

1 Prepare the board room for the Managing Directors' weekly meeting (10:00am start)
2 Distribute incoming mail to all staff
3 Type up an urgent 20-page report required by your section head
4 File documents
5 Re-arrange furniture and resources in the reception area
6 Prepare and send letters informing applicants of dates and times of interviews which will take place next week
7 Collect outgoing mail from all staff and prepare for posting
8 Prepare a PowerPoint presentation (ten slides) to be used by the Human Resources Manager in his presentation to staff in two days' time. Note that he wishes to check it first to make any necessary amendments

To ensure all tasks are completed on time and as efficiently as possible, prepare a priorities list.

Identify three possible time stealers that could impact on your workflow and suggest strategies you could use to prevent these.

DON'T FORGET

Targets should be SMART!

ONLINE

For more activities on setting targets, head to www.brightredbooks.net

ONLINE TEST

Head to www.brightredbooks.net and test your knowledge of setting targets.

CHANGING PRIORITIES AND MONITORING PROGRESS

DEALING WITH CHANGING PRIORITIES

Examples of circumstances that could affect day-to-day work/priorities include:

- a member of staff phoning in sick
- the computer network crashing
- a manager changing a deadline for a piece of work

Examples of circumstances that could affect the achievement of long-term targets include the following:

- A new supervisor may decide to take a different approach from that taken by their predecessor.
- Staff changes at senior management level have taken place.
- A new Chief Executive Officer (CEO) could decide to implement major changes that have a trickle-down effect.
- Restructuring, expansion or downsizing create changed priorities at all levels.

Examples of circumstances that could impact on the achievement of an individual employee's targets include the following:

- The targets were not SMART.
- The actions of others prevented the employee from being able to achieve the targets that had been set.
- The employee was requested to undertake additional tasks after targets and priorities were set.
- The employee was not equipped with the appropriate skills to achieve their targets.
- The line manager did not give the employee adequate support.

When a change in circumstances necessitates a change in priorities, it is important for employees to remain calm and solution-focused. Possible solutions could include:

- extending the deadline to complete tasks/achieve targets
- requesting overtime
- being assertive and saying no to additional work
- calling on additional help from other employees
- eliminating time stealers

MONITORING AND EVALUATING PROGRESS

There is no point in setting targets to improve time and task management if no-one bothers to keep to schedule to try and achieve them. Therefore certain controls must be put in place. Targets can be monitored in a variety of different ways. Managers may support their employees by checking at regular intervals that the work is progressing, or by putting a more experienced member of staff in charge to act as a mentor. Occasionally audits, which are really checks on systems and procedures, may take place as a project is ongoing or even when it is complete. A report would then be submitted to the manager with recommendations and a list of actions to be taken.

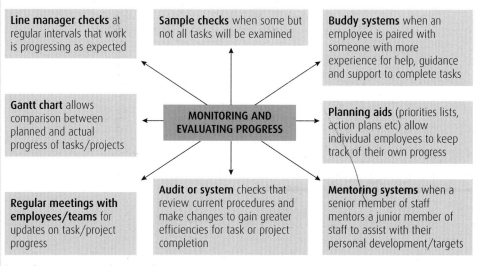

It is also important that employees are given opportunities to evaluate their performance on a regular basis, possibly through the staff appraisal process.

 THINGS TO DO AND THINK ABOUT

Exam-style questions

1 Justify the need for employees to develop good time management skills. 3 marks

2 Describe ways in which an Administrative Assistant would ensure that time is managed effectively. 6 marks

3 Identify two time stealers and outline one way of reducing the effect of each. 4 marks

4 Describe the implications of a manager who fails to delegate. 4 marks

5 Outline four features of effective targets. 4 marks

6 Describe two methods used by individuals to ensure their work targets are met. 4 marks

7 Outline ways in which an employee's targets can be monitored. 4 marks

8 Outline two skills and two qualities of an Administrative Assistant. 4 marks

9 Describe a situation within an organisation where a priority may have to change. 1 mark

10 Explain how good time/task management could benefit an organisation. 3 marks

11 Explain the consequences of poor time/task management. 3 marks

12 Outline two features of a personal development plan. 2 marks

 DON'T FORGET

Targets must be monitored and evaluated

 ONLINE

Check out the task on delegation at www.brightredbooks.net

 ONLINE TEST

Head to www.brightredbooks.net and test your knowledge of changing priorities and monitoring targets.

EFFECTIVE TEAMS 1

WHAT IS A TEAM?

A team can be defined as a group of people that has been specifically formed for a particular purpose or to achieve a particular aim. In recent years, as the structure of organisations has become flatter, team working has become much more common. A team is characterised by three main factors:

- a shared purpose or goal
- a shared identity
- a dependence/reliance on each member

In simple terms, an effective team will have good leadership and members who are keen to take on different roles. For example:

- taking responsibility for set tasks
- assisting the team leader to make decisions
- giving feedback at meetings and listening to other team members' ideas and suggestions
- helping and supporting other team members with their tasks
- offering opinions and suggestions and being prepared to compromise

ONLINE

For a great activity on team work, head to www.brightredbooks.net

VIDEO LINK

Go online and check out the clip at www.brightredbooks.net

DON'T FORGET

Belbin's nine team roles

TEAM FORMATION

Effective teams need to have a balance between the people who have the ideas and those who have the necessary skills to put them into action. If the team leader is able to identify these types of individuals when forming the team and is able to ensure a good balance, then it is likely to be easier to manage the relationships, behaviours and characteristics of the team.

It is also very important that careful consideration should be given to the size of a team. According to Meredith Belbin, a leading management theorist, teams of around four to six people are the most effective. If a team is too large there is a danger of sub-groups developing and if a team is too small there is a danger of one person dominating the team.

TEAM FORMATION

Meredith Belbin suggests that there are nine key roles within a team. These are outlined below:

BELBIN'S TEAM ROLES	
The Specialist	This is the person who has specialist expertise and/or skills.
The Ideas Person	The ideas person is creative, imaginative and has the ability to solve problems.
The Motivator	This is the person who has the courage to overcome obstacles and can drive the team forward.
The Organiser	The organiser can forward plan, co-ordinate activities, make decisions, delegate and pull things together.
The Implementer	This is the person who turns ideas into actions and is keen to get tasks started.
The Checker	The checker monitors and evaluates the work of the team and ensures that all tasks have been carried out correctly.
The Finisher	This is the person who keeps an eye on deadlines and ensures that all tasks are completed on time.
The Go-getter	The go-getter is the person who networks, develops contacts, explores opportunities and is able to access resources.
The Team Player	This is the person who cares about others in the team. The team player listens to others and tries to minimise conflict between team members.

Usually people are visibly strong in one role or another. Most people, however, are able to take on more than one role. For a team to be highly effective, it is important that there is a balance between 'thinkers' and 'doers'.

STAGES IN TEAM DEVELOPMENT

It is argued that before teams are fully effective they must go through four main stages. These are outlined in the table below:

Forming	Team members are selected and introduced to each other.
Storming	Members compete for roles within the team. There could be some disputes, competitiveness and power struggles as each member secures their role within the team.
Norming	Team members start working together to undertake tasks and/or solve problems. Any conflict is resolved at this stage.
Performing	The team is now settled and functioning highly effectively.

Some teams who have completed their assigned task or project will have a fifth stage called **adjourning**. The team will break up and team members may take on similar or new roles in another team undertaking a new project.

WHAT MAKES AN EFFECTIVE TEAM?

There are a number of factors that contribute to team effectiveness. These are:

- **Team membership** – When forming a team it is very important to consider factors such as the personality, interests, age and experience of potential team members.
- **Team development** – A group of employees who have experience of working with each other before and so know each other fairly well will develop more quickly.
- **Nature of the task** – Team members should believe in the task to be undertaken and want to contribute to its completion. The more involved the members feel, the more effective the team is likely to be.
- **Team maintenance** – It is very important that each team member identifies themselves as part of the team and is given the time and opportunity to develop as part of the team. Opportunities should be given both inside and outside the business for the team to take part in activities that foster team working.
- **Leadership** – It is important that a team has an effective leader who can motivate the team, minimise any conflict and support the team achieve its collective goals.
- **Conflict** – A team able to resolve conflict and move forward will be more effective.

TEAM CONFLICT

There are many reasons for conflict between team members. For example:

- **Conflicting goals** – when two team members want to go in opposite directions.
- **Personality clashes** – team members who just cannot get on with each other.
- **Changing expectations** – shortening deadlines or changing the targets or goals after the work has started is very likely to frustrate some team members.
- **Loyalty issues** – when cliques emerge among certain team members. Maintaining these friendships can then take priority over achieving team goals.
- **Lack of resources** – when team members have to compromise because there is not enough money, staff or equipment to turn all ideas into action.

The above issues are most likely to make the team less effective in achieving its goals.

THINGS TO DO AND THINK ABOUT

1. **Describe** three main factors that characterise a team.
2. **Explain** why it is important that teams are not too large or too small.
3. **Outline** the factors that should be considered when selecting team members.
4. **Outline** three factors that can cause conflict within a team.
5. An effective team should have a mixture of 'thinkers' and 'doers'. **Explain** the difference between a 'thinker' and a 'doer'.

VIDEO LINK

Head to www.brightredbooks.net to watch a clip on the stages of team development.

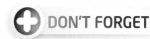
DON'T FORGET

There are four stages of team development

ONLINE TEST

Test yourself on effective teams at ww.brightredbooks.net

ONLINE

Head to www.brightredbooks.net and complete the case study.

DON'T FORGET

Conflict can reduce team effectiveness.

EFFECTIVE TEAMS 2

TEAM MEMBERS' SKILLS

Team members should possess three key skills. The more experience of team working that people have, the more refined these skills should become.

Leadership skills	Effective teams require a good leader. A good leader should motivate the team by setting a clear vision. A good leader will provide support to all members of the team, minimise conflict and provide opportunities for other team members to take on leadership roles for a specific aspect of the overall task.
Listening skills	All team members should be able to listen to each other's ideas and point of view.
Communication skills	All team members should be able to put their thoughts into words for everyone to understand. In simple terms, team members should be able to communicate both verbally and in writing

BENEFITS OF TEAMS TO INDIVIDUALS	BENEFITS OF TEAMS TO THE ORGANISATION
Increased morale and motivation	**Multi-skilled and flexible workforce**
There is a sense of being valued and belonging so individuals working in a team will have a greater sense of involvement. This can lead to increased motivation and job satisfaction.	Teams allow staff to be more flexible and to adapt to the needs of a business as required. For example, if a member of staff leaves the organisation or is absent, other members of the team can cover that person's duties between them.
Shared knowledge and skills	**Increased responsibility and less supervision**
Teams bring people together from a diverse range of backgrounds and expertise. Team members can therefore greatly benefit from sharing ideas, skills and knowledge with one another. This can help develop an individual's role within an organisation.	Team work creates a sense of interdependence between team members and encourages team members to take on additional responsibility. As a result, teams require less supervision which could result in fewer layers of management being necessary, reducing costs for the organisation.
Risk-taking	**Increased productivity**
Decisions made by a team means that no one person takes full responsibility for decisions. Teams are therefore more likely to try out new (and perhaps riskier) ideas that an individual employee may have been reluctant to suggest. No individual employee is held accountable for a decision that did not go to plan.	As a result of increased morale, motivation and sharing of expertise, the organisation is likely to benefit from increased productivity. There is also likely to be a reduction in staff turnover, reducing recruitment and training costs.
Sense of being valued and belonging	**Risk-taking**
Being invited to be part of a team increases an individual's feeling of self-worth, and professional recognition within a business.	As teams are more likely to take risks, this can give an organisation a competitive edge.

TEAM LEADERSHIP

Good leaders generally have the ability to think clearly, analyse situations and make decisions. In addition, they know how to delegate tasks, motivate employees and communicate to a high standard – both in writing and verbally. They have very good social skills and can build relationships with all members of their team. Instead of having to coerce followers, a good leader will motivate employees to achieve their goals. There are different forms of leadership but in most modern organisations the democratic leader is the preferred style.

Types of leadership

Autocratic	The leader makes all the decisions without consultation and with little regard for the thoughts and opinions of other employees.
Democratic	The leader is much more consultative and seeks the views and thoughts of other employees. Participative decision-making is encouraged.
Laissez-faire	This is a kind of distributed leadership. Here, the leader prefers the workforce to make their own decisions, particularly when they work in teams and have specialist insight into a particular area.

contd

DON'T FORGET

Teams provide benefits for both individual team members and the organisation.

VIDEO LINK

Go online and watch the presentation at www.brightredbooks.net

DON'T FORGET

The Administrative Assistant is likely to work as part of a team when planning and organising business events and conferences.

VIDEO LINK

Head to www.brightredbooks.net and watch the presentation.

DON'T FORGET

A good leader will motivate rather than coerce others.

The kind of leadership required by a team will depend on three main factors:

1 Is the team new or is it established?

2 Is the team experienced and highly effective?

3 Is the task risky and complex or straightforward?

In a new and less experienced team, it will be necessary for the leader to take more of a directing role. An established and more experienced team will require a leader who is more of a facilitator. An established team will work together, support one another and willingly take responsibility. As a result there will be less need for the leader to direct the team.

Benefits of good leadership

A team that is led by a highly effective leader who demonstrates commitment, displays honesty and accepts accountability will bring about the following benefits:

- increased participation, motivation and job satisfaction for all members of the team

- clearly defined aims and objectives for the team, which should lead to quicker achievement of goals or increased productivity

- open two-way communication between the leader and team members, encouraging greater participation and so facilitating the exchange of more ideas among all team members

- greater chance of the team's work being accepted without question when the leader has established their expertise and integrity

- better career prospects for all team members because they will have developed as individual employees thanks to good leadership

- improved communication and collaborative working, which will lead to better decision-making

ONLINE

Head to www.brightredbooks.net for further activities on effective teamwork.

ONLINE TEST

Test your knowledge of effective teamwork at www.brightredbooks.net

THINGS TO DO AND THINK ABOUT

Short answer questions

1 State any two skills that team members should possess.

2 Outline the benefits to an individual from being part of a team.

3 Describe the benefits to an organisation from using teams.

4 Outline three styles of leadership that could be adopted by a team leader.

5 Outline the benefits to team members when they are led by a highly effective leader

Exam-style questions

1 Explain the advantages to the individual and organisation of working as part of a team.   6 marks

2 Describe the benefits of good team leadership within a team.   4 marks

3 Describe the features of an effective team.   6 marks

4 Describe the ways a team can be affected by poor leadership.   6 marks

5 Describe any three roles from Belbin's theory of teams.   3 marks

6 'Successful teams need effective leaders'. Outline four qualities of an effective leader.   4 marks

7 Describe the benefits of an effective team.   6 marks

8 Explain why some teams are more effective than others.   4 marks

HEALTH AND SAFETY LEGISLATION 1

All work exposes people to hazards. Attention to **health and safety** is not just about being socially responsible; it makes good business sense.

DON'T FORGET

The Health and Safety at Work Act 1974 is known as an 'umbrella act'.

DON'T FORGET

The HASAWA 1974 places legal responsibilities on both employers and employees.

DON'T FORGET

Account should always be taken of health and safety legislation when planning and organising business events and conferences.

DON'T FORGET

HASAWA is the main piece of health and safety legislation in the UK.

VIDEO LINK

Go to www.brightredbooks. net and watch the short video clip on HASAWA.

HEALTH AND SAFETY AT WORK ACT 1974

Health and safety legislation relating to the workplace is constantly being updated. It is important that all staff in business organisations know the main provisions of the **Health and Safety at Work Act 1974** (HASAWA). The HASWA is an 'umbrella act'; that is, it contains a number of other acts, each covering specific aspects of health and safety. It is also known as an 'enabling act', meaning that it allows for any new acts or amendments to be added.

The HASAWA provides broad statements in relation to minimum health and safety requirements and places legal responsibilities on both employers and employees.

Employers must:

- provide a safe place of work for employees
- ensure that entrances and exits are clearly marked
- provide safe equipment and machinery and ensure that it is regularly checked and maintained
- provide training to employees on health and safety in the workplace
- display information on health and safety in the workplace on notice boards
- provide a written health and safety policy, which is kept up to date and available to all staff
- communicate clear procedures for dealing with accidents in the workplace and ensure all accidents are accurately recorded
- provide a safety representative to represent employees' needs.

Employees must:

- co-operate with health and safety policies and take all reasonable care of themselves and other employees
- immediately report any faults with machinery or equipment
- wear protective clothing when it has been issued to them
- always follow guidelines when operating machinery and equipment and never operate machinery or equipment they are not authorised or trained to use
- co-operate with their employer by attending training courses
- ensure they are familiar with the organisation's health and safety policy
- be observant and report any hazards in the workplace.

The most prominent pieces of legislation contained in the Health and Safety at Work Act are:

Reporting of Injuries, Diseases and Dangerous Occurrences Regulations (RIDDOR) 1995

This deals specifically with the reporting of injuries and accidents at work (serious and fatal).

- Accidents must be reported when they result in an employee or self-employed person being away from work or unable to perform their normal work duties for more than seven consecutive days as the result of their injury.
- Accidents must be recorded, but not reported, when they result in a worker being incapacitated for more than three consecutive days.
- Accidents to members of the public or others who are not at work must be reported if they result in an injury and the person is taken directly from the scene of the accident to hospital for treatment for that injury.

contd

Control of Substances Hazardous to Health (COSHH) 1994

This deals specifically with the storage and control of hazardous substances and items such as protective equipment and clothing.

COSHH requires employers to control substances that are hazardous to health. Employers can prevent or reduce workers' exposure to hazardous substances by:

- finding out what the health hazards are
- deciding how to prevent harm to health
- providing control measures to reduce harm to health
- providing information, instruction and training for employees and others
- providing monitoring and health surveillance in appropriate cases
- planning for emergencies.

Health and Safety (First Aid) Regulations 1981

These require employers to provide adequate and appropriate equipment, facilities and personnel to ensure their employees receive immediate attention if they are injured or taken ill at work. These regulations apply to all workplaces, including those with fewer than five employees, and to the self-employed.

What is 'adequate and appropriate' will depend on the circumstances in the workplace. This includes whether trained first-aiders are needed, what should be included in a first-aid box and if a first-aid room is required. Employers should carry out an assessment of first-aid needs to determine what to provide.

The Regulations do not place a legal duty on employers to make first-aid provision for non-employees such as the public. However, it is strongly recommended that non-employees are included in an assessment of first-aid needs and that provision is made for them.

Workplace (Health, Safety and Welfare) Regulations 1992

These cover the four main areas of the workplace – the working environment, safety, facilities (for example, toilets) and maintenance of equipment and premises. Examples include:

- The workplace and equipment are in good working order and in good repair.
- Effective and suitable ventilation should be provided.
- The temperature inside the workplace is reasonable and thermometers are provided for employees.
- No method of cooling or heating which results in the escape of fumes, gases or vapours likely to be injurious or offensive shall be used.
- Lighting, as far as is practicable, should be natural.
- The workplace, the surfaces and the furniture, furnishings and fittings should be clean.
- Waste should not accumulate.
- The room dimensions should be reasonable to ensure good health, safety and welfare.
- Where the nature of the work deems it appropriate, a suitable and sufficient supply of the following must be provided:
  - washing facilities including showers
  - accommodation for work clothes
  - facilities for changing clothes
  - facilities for rest and for eating meals
  - an adequate supply of safe drinking water

THINGS TO DO AND THINK ABOUT

Short response questions

1. The Health and Safety at Work Act 1974 is known as an 'umbrella act'. What does this mean?
2. What responsibilities does the Health and Safety at Work Act place on employers?
3. List some responsibilities that the Health and Safety at Work Act places on employees.
4. Why do you think that health and safety should be a key business objective?

DON'T FORGET

Accidents which result in seven days' absence from work should be reported to the Health and Safety Executive.

ONLINE TEST

Test yourself on health and safety legislation at www.brightredbooks.net

ONLINE

Head to www.brightredbooks.net and read examples of organisations who have not adhered to the Health and Safety at Work Act.

HEALTH AND SAFETY LEGISLATION 2

THE HEALTH AND SAFETY (DISPLAY SCREEN EQUIPMENT) REGULATIONS 1992

Components of a comfortable workstation

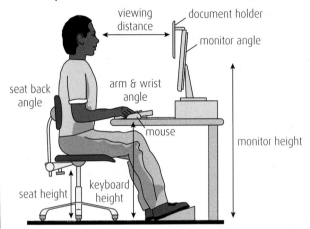

These regulations provide protection for employees working at workstations with VDUs and PCs. They give guidance on the length of time to work at a VDU and advice on the provision of special equipment such as screen and wrist guards to avoid fatigue or strains. Employers must:

- examine workstations and ensure that they are suitable for the work to be carried out
- ensure that workstations meet minimum requirements: the VDU can be adjusted for brightness and contrast; adjustable chairs are provided; footrests are provided if requested; keyboards can be adjusted and are separate from the screen
- ensure that employees are given suitable breaks or can change activity away from the VDU
- provide eye tests if the employee requests this and provide glasses or contact lenses if special ones are needed for VDU work
- provide health and safety training and information to employees to ensure VDUs and workstations are used safely.

ONLINE

Go to www.brightredbooks. net and watch the short video for more on health and safety.

THE FIRE (SCOTLAND) ACT 2005

Most fires are preventable. Those responsible for workplaces and other buildings to which the public has access can avoid them by taking responsibility for and adopting the right behaviours and procedures.

Employers must carry out a fire safety risk assessment and keep it up to date. This can be carried out either as part of an overall risk assessment or as a separate exercise. The risk assessment looks at the premises, the activities carried out there, and the potential for a fire to occur and the harm it could cause.

DUTIES OF EMPLOYER	DUTIES OF EMPLOYEES
Identify the people at risk	Take care of their own safety in respect of harm caused by fire
Identify the fire hazards	Take care of other people who may be affected by acts of the employee
Evaluate risk and decide if existing fire safety measures are adequate	Co-operate with employer with respect to fire legislation
Record the risk assessment undertaken and review at regular intervals	

THE 'SIX-PACK'

As the UK is part of the European Union, it has to take account of certain EU regulations. In 1993, six European Health and Safety directives were enforced in Britain. These become known as the 'Six-pack' and covered key aspects of health and safety legislation including safe use of work equipment, manual handling and management of health and safety at work. Two main additions from this European legislation are:

- the requirement for employers to carry out regular risk assessments
- increased employee participation with health and safety matters.

BREACHES OF HEALTH AND SAFETY LEGISLATION

Health and Safety Executive

If an organisation does not follow health and safety guidelines then the Health and Safety Executive (HSE) – the national body responsible for the enforcement of health and safety – or local government Environmental Health departments can:

- enter and inspect premises – sometimes unannounced
- issue improvement notices and provide advice
- question and interview people and give warnings
- shut down premises without notice
- fine or prosecute when necessary.

In addition, employees who believe that the organisation has breached health and safety requirements can take their case to an industrial tribunal. Examples might be the non-provision of safety equipment/protective clothing or failure to 'remedy' a reported hazard, which has resulted in subsequent injury. If a case is proven against the employer, it may result in fines or in compensation to the employee.

An employee failing to comply with health and safety policies could face a number of disciplinary procedures:

- a verbal warning
- a written warning
- suspension
- a fine
- dismissal
- criminal or civil prosecution

It is an employer's responsibility to provide information to employees on health and safety legislation. Most business organisations will have a formal written health and safety policy. However, it is very important that this information is communicated to all employees to ensure it is put into practice.

Training	When an employee starts working with the organisation they should be issued with a copy of the health and safety policy as part of their induction training. It is important that staff are kept up to date on a regular basis on health and safety issues, including training in the use of any new equipment.
Company intranet	The company intranet can be used to pass on key information to staff as all staff will have access to information stored in a central area.
Noticeboards	Posters can be displayed on noticeboards to remind staff about procedures such as fire drills and first-aid procedures.
Demonstrations	Demonstrations can be used for practical activities such as fire drills or first-aid procedures. They can also be used for training small groups of staff on how to operate machines and equipment.
Staff meetings	If information regarding health and safety policies is required to be given to all staff then a meeting is the quickest and most efficient way to ensure that information is conveyed to all staff.
Health and safety Representatives	These are trained employees who should be available for advice and can provide information to employees. Health and safety representatives can raise issues with employers that employees have concerns about.

THINGS TO DO AND THINK ABOUT

Researching and presenting information

You are the Administrative Assistant in the Human Resources Department at Johnstone's PLC. The Human Resources Manager, Mr Graeme Keen, is planning on giving a talk next week to all staff regarding the importance of health and safety legislation.

He has asked you to prepare a PowerPoint presentation (for his approval) to be used when meeting with staff next week. He wants it to focus on the following:

- Health and Safety at Work Act 1974 (and other key acts/pieces of legislation that come under Health and Safety)
- Duties of employers/employees
- Penalties for breaching Health and Safety legislation

The presentation should be no more than 12 slides. Print a draft copy of your presentation in handout form in order that Mr Keen can check it.

You may wish to visit the following website to assist you with this task: http://www.inbrief.co.uk/employees/health-and-safety-at-work-act.htm

 **DON'T FORGET**

The Health and Safety Executive (HSE) is the national body for enforcing health and safety legislation.

HSE
Health & Safety Executive

 ONLINE TEST

Head to ww.brightredbooks.net to test yourself on health and safety.

 DON'T FORGET

The issue of health and safety is a very serious one for both employers and employees and failure to comply with either legislation or organisational procedures can result in heavy penalties for all concerned.

 DON'T FORGET

Organisations have a responsibility to keep staff up-to-date on health and safety issues.

 ONLINE

Head to www.brightredbooks.net for more activities on this topic.

DATA-HANDLING LEGISLATION

With more and more organisations using computers to store and process personal information there is a danger that the information could be misused or fall into the wrong hands. To address these concerns, the UK government introduced legislation to govern data handling. Other European Union countries have passed similar laws as often information is held in more than one country.

DON'T FORGET

When planning business events and conferences the Administrative Assistant must ensure that data protection legislation is adhered to at all times.

DON'T FORGET

A user is the person (or organisation) controlling the data and the way in which it is being used. A subject is the person to whom the data refers.

VIDEO LINK

Go to www.brightredbooks. net and watch the video clip on this.

DON'T FORGET

Serious breaches of the Data Protection Act can result in fines of up to £500 000.

DON'T FORGET

Organisations must ensure all possible measures are taken to protect personal information.

THE DATA PROTECTION ACT 1984 AND 1988

This law was created in 1984 to protect computer-based information but was amended in 1998 to cover paper-based information too.

Data users must register with the Data Protection Registrar so that they can monitor the:

- nature of the data (WHAT)
- reason for the data being kept (WHY)
- method used to collect the data (HOW)
- parties/people data will be passed on to (WHO).

If an organisation is dealing with personal data they must adhere to the principles of good practice. These state that personal data:

- should be obtained fairly and lawfully
- shall be used for the registered purpose only
- shall not be disclosed for any other reason than is given to the Registrar
- shall be relevant, adequate and not excessive for the purpose
- must be accurate and kept up to date
- shall not be kept for longer than is needed
- should be available to the data subject and should be changed if it is not accurate
- should be secure: there must be steps taken to keep it safe from unauthorised access or from being lost.

If an organisation goes against these principles or fails to register with the Registrar, they may face a number of consequences.

Monetary penalty notices	Fines of up to £500 000 can be issued for serious breaches of the Data Protection Act.
Undertakings	Organisations have to commit to a particular course of action to improve their compliance with the legislation and avoid further action from the Information Commissioner's Office (ICO).
Enforcement notices	Organisations in breach of the Data Protection Act are instructed to take specific steps in order to comply with the law. There will be strict monitoring to ensure enforcement notices are executed in full.
Audit	The ICO has the power to audit government departments without consent.

Subjects who feel the data stored about them is not accurate can complain or request compensation for any distress caused.

Organisations must look at ways of protecting data and could use a number of these rules:

1	All staff should be issued with their own username and password – passwords should be changed regularly.	7	Every effort must be made to ensure that the information they hold on individuals or businesses is accurate and up to date.
2	All employees should use a password-protected screen saver or lock the screen when not at their desk.	8	Action should be taken to prevent physical threats, for example theft. Organisations should ensure that buildings are locked and alarmed, security-marking equipment and enforcing formal procedures for entry to and exit from the building.
3	Sensitive information should not be stored on USBs or pen drives. These are easily lost and could end up in the hands of others who could use them for criminal activities.	9	Original software should be stored securely and there should be formal back-up procedures for all data.
4	Sensitive information should be disposed of in a safe and responsible manner – information held on paper should be shredded.	10	Access rights should be used. An employee's log-in should determine the level of access they have. Those in a higher position should be given more access to information than a junior member of staff.
5	Anti-virus software should be installed on all computers.	11	All paper-based information must also be kept secure by making use of locked filing cabinets in secure areas.
6	Information must not be shared with other individuals or organisations who do not have the right to access it.	12	Paper files that are no longer needed should be shredded.

COMPUTER MISUSE ACT 1990

This law was created when computers were being introduced to more businesses. It prohibits unlawful access to computer systems. The Act makes it illegal to:

- access computers/computer systems without permission (hacking)
- access computers with the intention of committing a criminal offence (for example, introducing a virus)
- access computers to change or alter details in the system without permission (copying details/software).

COPYRIGHT, DESIGNS AND PATENTS ACT 1988

Copyright is the right of an author to control and benefit from their work. Copyright is shown by a © next to the name of the owner and the words 'all rights reserved' or 'no part of this publication may be reproduced without permission'. The Act seeks to ensure that no unauthorised copying takes place, be it of books, music or computer programs. To reproduce any material under copyright, a user needs to seek the owner's permission and may be asked to pay a fee. A user can also pay a fee to the Copyright Licensing Agency which will allow them to copy small sections without permission.

VIDEO LINK

Head to www.brightredbooks.net and check out the short video clip.

FREEDOM OF INFORMATION ACT 2000

The Freedom of Information Act provides public access to information held by public authorities. This means that:

- public authorities are obliged to publish certain information about their activities
- members of the public are entitled to request information from public authorities.

ONLINE TEST

Test yourself on data-handling legislation at www.brightredbooks.net

FAILING TO COMPLY WITH HEALTH AND SAFETY AND/OR DATA HANDLING LEGISLATION

Customers lose confidence in the organisation and may not want to do business with them
Competitors may gain a competitive edge if they become more attractive to customers
The organisation may face legal procedures and financial penalties for non-compliance
High-profile incidents covered by the media may result in negative publicity
The organisation may develop a bad reputation
Sales and profits may fall

ONLINE

For further activities on this topic, head to www.brightredbooks.net

 THINGS TO DO AND THINK ABOUT

Exam-style questions

1 Describe the key responsibilities employers have with regard to display screen equipment regulations. **4 marks**

2 Describe ways in which an organisation can inform employees about workplace legislation. **4 marks**

3 Describe the consequences for an employee if they breach health and safety legislation. **3 marks**

4 Outline the main features of the Data Protection Act. **3 marks**

5 Outline the main features of the Freedom of Information Act. **2 marks**

6 Outline two offences under the Computer Misuse Act 1990 **2 marks**

7 Outline four rights of the individual as outlined in the Data Protection Act. **4 marks**

IMPACT OF ICT ON WORKING PRACTICES

The work environment has changed greatly in the last 20 years. The building of any new work premises will take environmental factors into account and will be designed to make the best and most flexible use of the available space. It is much more common now to find people working in large open-plan offices rather than smaller, traditional cellular offices (one or two people working in their own space or room bounded by permanent walls).

VIDEO LINK

Go to www.brightredbooks. net and observe the following video comparing office layouts.

DON'T FORGET

There are two main types of office – cellular and open-plan.

VIDEO LINK

Go to www.brightredbooks. net and observe the following video showing the layout of a modern, environmentally friendly open-plan office.

ONLINE

Head to www.brightredbooks. net for a case study on office layouts.

OFFICE LAYOUT

The layout and condition of the office will affect work in a number of ways. A poorly designed layout will disrupt the efficiency of the workflow. Employees who work in large open-plan environments sometimes complain of headaches, sore throats and fatigue, which they believe to be associated with the building they work in – poor layout, ventilation, lighting or even decor. This is known as **sick building syndrome**.

Example of a large, modern open-plan office.

Open-plan office

An open-plan layout can be totally open (without any kind of partition of space at all) or 'landscaped', which is more often the case. Landscaped layouts will use plants, furniture and partitions/screens to create work areas within one large space.

ADVANTAGES	DISADVANTAGES
Easy to supervise	Can be noisy with lots of distractions
Savings in space and equipment can be shared	Unable to alter heating or lighting to suit personal requirements – there is often only air conditioning
Staff do not feel isolated – sociable layout or social areas away from work areas	Lack of privacy
Meeting rooms for private work	Does not give status of 'own office'
Shared resources, for example paper-based files	
Can be designed to suit workflow and teamwork	

Cellular office

This type of layout consists of individual offices accommodating one or two employees

ADVANTAGES	DISADVANTAGES
Quiet – doors can be closed	Wastes space
Status – boss has own room	More difficult to supervise
Privacy for one-to-one discussions	More difficult to share resources
Ability to alter heat and light to suit personal requirements	Uneconomic with regard to lighting/heating
Office can be personalised	Employees may feel isolated
	Difficult to promote team work

ERGONOMICS

Office **ergonomics** is about fitting the workspace environment and the employee together in the best way to prevent physical and mental health problems. Increased use of technology means that more employees use workstations with PCs and VDUs, resulting in an increase in musculoskeletal disorders. These are conditions which involve muscles or the skeleton and include carpal tunnel syndrome, repetitive strain injuries, back injuries, neck and shoulder pain.

contd

Ergonomics can help prevent, alleviate or even treat some of these conditions. The right type of furniture and equipment, lighting, ventilation, decor, pictures, plants and personal possessions in the right place can help to create a feeling of well-being in the workplace.

premises and decor

lighting

heating

noise

equipment, furniture and storage

layout

Features of an ergonomically designed environment which is comfortable to the majority of workers and takes account of individual needs, health and safety issues and legislation include:

- suitable, comfortable and adjustable furniture
- wall colours which create a relaxed mood
- suitable lighting and ventilation
- noise control through the use of double glazing and appropriate floor coverings
- workstations which offer space and privacy
- protective equipment such as wrist-rests and anti-glare screens.

A well-designed, well-laid-out ergonomic environment reduces the risk of sick building syndrome and has a huge impact on both the individual and the organisation by:

- improving morale and motivation and helping productivity
- ensuring effective flow of work
- promoting health and safety at work
- giving a positive image for the organisation
- being cost-effective as a result of the above.

Office layout should also contribute to productive and efficient **workflow**. Workflow describes the flow of people and paper around the office. If the layout leads to unnecessary movement around the building and results in delays, hold-ups and frustration then there is a problem with the workplace design. Good design principles include:

- siting associated work areas together, for example, sales and purchasing
- no unnecessary physical barriers to get from A to B
- common services/equipment sited centrally for all to use.

DON'T FORGET

A good ergonomic environment reduces the risk of sick building syndrome.

FLEXIBLE WORKING PRACTICES

Developments in ICT have resulted in a large number of people being able to carry out homeworking and teleworking thanks to better methods of communication. Video and audio conferencing have also made it possible for people in remote locations to have meetings without the need to travel. In addition, working practices have had to change to fit in with modern lifestyles. The traditional 9 to 5 working hours have been replaced with more flexible options for both the employer and the employee. There have been changes in society that have led to a different type of workforce. These include:

- more women returning to the workplace after having children
- more entrepreneurs setting up their own business but choosing to work part-time in another job for security
- more people undertaking full-time higher/further education courses combined with part-time employment
- more people seeking a better work–life balance.

VIDEO LINK

Check out the clips about flexible working practices at www.brightredbooks.net

THINGS TO DO AND THINK ABOUT

1 Outline the advantages and disadvantages of an open-plan office.
2 Explain what is meant by a cellular office.
3 Explain what is meant by the term office ergonomics.
4 Outline some of the features associated with sick building syndrome.
5 Outline the features that should be taken into consideration when designing a positive ergonomic office environment.

WORKING PRACTICES

Different working practices that organisations might operate are outlined in the table below.

Type of contract	Permanent, temporary, fixed-term
Working hours	Full-time, part-time, flexitime, job-share
Mode of work	Office-based, homeworking, teleworking, hot desking

TYPE OF CONTRACT

Full-time

Employees work on average 35–40 hours per week, usually from 9:00am to 5:00pm, five days per week. The average full-time working week in the UK is the longest in Europe!

Part-time

The employee's basic hours are less than full time. The number of hours and the days of the week worked will vary and depend on what is agreed between the employer and the employee. Part-time employees are entitled to the same wage rates, working conditions and benefits received by full-time employees but they receive them on a **pro rata** basis – work half the week, get half the pay.

WORKING HOURS

Flexitime

Employees can choose when they start and finish work. There are **core hours** when all employees must be at work. These are usually the busy periods, for example 10:00am–12:00pm and 2:00pm–4:00pm. Employees can choose their own start and finish times outwith the core times so long as they work their contracted number of hours for the week or month. Employees can accumulate flexi days by building up a number of additional hours worked during the month and then taking the equivalent days off later. If the employee is working on a long, complicated task they can continue without interruption knowing they can adjust their hours accordingly later.

Job-share

This is when two people share one job, splitting the hours between them. For example, Jo might work Monday, Tuesday and Wednesday morning. Pat will then finish the week by working Wednesday afternoon, Thursday and Friday. The hours can be split to suit the individuals who are sharing the job. Pay and benefits are also shared. It is very important that they keep in contact so that each knows what the other has done.

MODE OF WORKING

Homeworking

Employees are able to work from home, giving them the advantages of saving time that would normally be spent travelling, having greater flexibility to choose when they work and allowing their job to fit in with their lifestyle. However the downside of homeworking is that there may be a loss of social contact and the employee may miss out on training opportunities.

Teleworking

Employees are able to work away from the office – for example, on a train, on a plane, while staying in a hotel on business – and stay in touch with the office via technology such as e-mail, Skype or mobile phone.

Hot desking

If many employees work away from the office, there may be no need to have a desk or

DON'T FORGET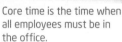

Core time is the time when all employees must be in the office.

DON'T FORGET

A job can be shared in a ratio that suits the individual employees.

DON'T FORGET

People working out of the office must ensure they comply with data protection legislation.

contd

office for each person. Instead, employees can use any desk that is free when they need it and can book a time slot to use a hot desk when they know they will be in the office. A hot desk will usually be equipped with a telephone and a PC so that employees can access their work. When they have finished working they have to clear away their files and leave the area completely free for whoever uses the hot desk next.

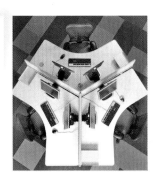

Touchdown areas

Employees who work away from the office a lot may need to come into the office for a short time. They may just need to send a quick e-mail or read a document. A touchdown area does not need to be booked and is less formal than a hot desk. It may be a seating area with a Wi-Fi connection for laptops.

CAREER BREAKS

Different organisations offer different types of breaks. The most common examples are when women take time out to have a family or employees take an extended break to go travelling. The length of the break may vary according to the employee and the organisation.

Unpaid leave

If an employee wishes to take a certain amount of time off but has already used their full annual leave entitlement, the company may allow them to take the time off but they will not receive pay. For example, an employee may require time off work to care for an ill relative.

ONLINE

For some great activities and case studies on working practices, head to www.brightredbooks.net

ONLINE TEST

Test yourself on this topic at www.brightredbooks.net

CASE STUDY

Working from home – Martin Catchpole

In 2008 I found myself facing redundancy for the first time in my career. Once I had recovered from the shock, I started to look at the job market to see what was available for me. I had looked at homeworking on and off for many years. Although I was sceptical at first, I decided to take a look at the new opportunity available from Arise for home-based call centre work that was heading to the UK after its success in the US.

In my previous role as a contact centre manager I had, over the years, worked alongside some smaller homeworking companies. Technology was advancing and I realised that this particular market was growing and had a huge amount of potential to change people's lives, creating a better standard of living and a more enjoyable work–life balance. As soon as I chose to partner with Arise, I knew that life would never be the same again and I am pleased to say that I am still enjoying the experience just as much as ever!

When I consider the savings I have made from working from home I am astounded. I have saved 4·5 hours' travelling time per week – that's nearly half a day in commuting alone! Wear and tear on the car has been reduced significantly. I have reduced my annual mileage from 18 000 miles to just 900. The reduction in mileage has also reduced my insurance premium. The cost of fuel has risen significantly over the years and now I can enjoy these savings too. When you factor all these savings in, you can see that the potential income saved by working from home rises quite significantly.

However, the best thing about working from home is having the time to see the children have all their 'firsts'. Being able to do the school run and spend time with them adds a priceless element to my quality of life.

Questions

1   What are the main advantages, according to Martin Catchpole, of working from home?
2   What ICT equipment would be necessary to enable someone to work from home?
3   Suggest one possible disadvantage to an employee of working from home.

THINGS TO DO AND THINK ABOUT

1   State one advantage to employer and one to employee of homeworking.
2   Explain the main difference between a hot desk and a touchdown area.
3   Core time is one condition of an employee working flexi-time. Explain what is meant by core time.

THE IMPACT OF NEW WORK PRACTICES 1

DON'T FORGET

Flexible working practices create advantages and disadvantages for both employer and employee.

ADVANTAGES AND DISADVANTAGES

Flexible working practices offer a number of advantages and disadvantages to both the employer and the employee. These are outlined in the tables below.

Employer

ADVANTAGES TO EMPLOYER	DISADVANTAGES TO EMPLOYER
Contracts of employment can be issued for the hours employees are required so there is a larger pool of labour with a wider range of skills	It can be difficult and costly to offer training and staff development to all part-time workers
Being able to offer flexible work patterns may suit employees with children, therefore good staff can be retained and the need to recruit and train new employees reduced	It is not always easy to ensure health and safety practices are being adhered to in the home environment or other locations
Happier staff will lead to improved morale and motivation and increased productivity	It is harder to organise and control a large number of part-time workers
Less absenteeism	Difficulties in communication
Savings through cheaper rent/accommodation costs as reduced building space and less equipment is required	Technical difficulties when ICT equipment breaks down
Short-term contracts can be used to employ staff only when they are needed (especially useful in businesses where demand for their goods/services is seasonal).	
Organisations can buy in specialist skills for short-term projects without incurring the need to train/retrain their existing staff	

Employee

ADVANTAGES TO EMPLOYEE	DISADVANTAGES TO EMPLOYEE
Flexible work patterns make it easier to combine work and family life, especially for single parents or carers	There might be fewer opportunities for staff development and training
Part-time workers tend to have lower stress levels as they have some time to recharge their batteries on days off	Employees can feel isolated when working in the home environment
Freedom to choose when and where to work	Hot-desking may result in a depersonalisation of space, leading to a feeling of not belonging to the organisation
Reduction in travel	It can be more difficult to develop new relationships
More accessible for people with disabilities	Difficult to balance work and home commitments. Employees need to be disciplined to work when in their own home
In the long term, employees can benefit from improved skills and experience, having been able to stay with the same organisation for a longer period.	Question of job security if contracts are increasingly of a temporary or fixed-term nature – there are implications with regard to pensions and ability to secure a mortgage.

ADVANCING TECHNOLOGIES AND FLEXIBLE WORKING PRACTICES

Developments in the internet, mobile phones and smartphones, webcams, and video and audio conferencing mean that individuals can work collaboratively without physically being in the same room. Technology such as Skype and FaceTime has developed this further, giving employees the ability to hold meetings in which each attendee is in a different location.

ADVANTAGES OF TECHNOLOGY ADVANCES	DISADVANTAGES OF TECHNOLOGY ADVANCES
Meetings can take place around the world without people having to travel, which saves time and money. In addition, more employees can work 'away' from the organisation.	Some people may feel awkward in front of a camera and still prefer a face-to-face meeting.
Using Skype or FaceTime is more personal than telephone calls and allows people to see each other and observe body language and other non-verbal cues, leading to increased clarity.	If there is a network fault or the system crashes then the meeting will have to be postponed.
Demonstrations can be given online and files can be exchanged.	Management and supervision of employees' work and the number of hours worked becomes more difficult.

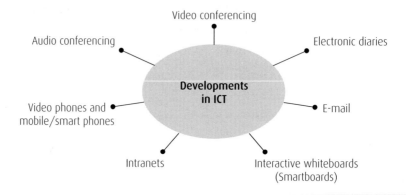

COMMUNICATION

Communication in the traditional office was mainly paper-based (in the form of letters and memos). In the modern office, as working practices have become more flexible and ICT continues to develop at a rapid pace, communication is mainly electronic. The diagram on p112 summarises the main forms of communication in today's office.

Mobile phones/Smartphones/Videophone

Mobile phones have become essential tools for keeping in touch with colleagues, but perhaps their biggest influence has been in the growth of text messaging. This is now one of the most common methods of communication, but it may encourage poor spelling, and may have a negative effect on the use of proper business language.

Mobile phones can allow the user to send and receive calls and messages, store messages, use voicemail, take and receive photos and small movies and surf the internet. They are invaluable for the businessperson who has to travel away from the office regularly as they can be used almost anywhere (although some areas have poor or no reception).

Many organisations now have a mobile phone policy which usually states that the mobile should be on silent or vibrate mode and that personal calls should not be made or received during working hours.

E-mail

E-mail is an extremely quick way to communicate and most e-mail accounts can also be used through mobile phones. E-mail is now the most commonly used method of communication in large offices today.

Instant messaging

Instant messaging (IM) involves exchanging messages with someone in real time over the internet. It is like a telephone conversation but using text instead of speech.

Wikis

This is a collection of articles on the internet that users can add to and edit freely.

ADVANTAGES OF E-MAIL	DISADVANTAGES OF E-MAIL
Fast way of sending information and so speeds up communication	Storage issues – limited size of inbox
Information is sent electronically so costs of paper and printing are reduced so more environmentally friendly	Network problems can delay communication and impact on workflow
Files can be attached to e-mails	Danger of sending e-mails to the wrong person can breach data handling legislation and/or cause embarrassment
Can create permanent records of who sent correspondence and when	Time stealer – employees may try to use e-mail for personal correspondence and this can reduce productivity
E-mail can be accessed anywhere with internet connection	Possible introduction of viruses to a computer system especially when attachments have been included in the e-mail
Same message can be sent to many people	
Delivery receipts and read receipts can be used as proof that someone actually received and read a message	
Good method of communication when working across time zones – allows 24/7 communication	
Reduces the need for office storage space.	

Blogs

A blog is a type of online personal journal or diary in which the author (the 'blogger') expresses themselves to the world about a particular subject that they are especially interested in or, more generally, about their everyday life. Blogs are usually updated frequently – as often as every day – and the content is archived so that anyone can look through old blog entries or search for certain words or themes.

THINGS TO DO AND THINK ABOUT

What reasons would you give to a reluctant Chief Executive Officer (CEO) to convince them to introduce flexible working practices?

ONLINE TEST

Head to www.brightredbooks.net and take the topic test.

ONLINE

For some great activities and case studies on the impact of new working practices, head to www.brightredbooks.net

THE IMPACT OF NEW WORK PRACTICES 2

DON'T FORGET

Video conference facilities can be hired.

COMMUNICATION

Video conferencing

This method of communication has revolutionised the way meetings are now held. Nearly all large organisations have video conferencing facilities; these usually consist of a large television/plasma screen, a computer network and video conferencing software. The facilities must be available at all organisations taking part in the video conference. The link allows two or more groups of people in different parts of the country (or even the world) to meet and discuss business without having the problems and costs of travel and accommodation. This saves an enormous amount of time and money and has been very successful in improving communication in large multinational companies. Companies that do not have video conferencing facilities can hire the service from a company or supplier.

Intranet

Many companies have their own intranet, which is a private network that can be accessed by the staff but not by anyone outside the company. Companies generally use their intranet for storing policies and procedures, forms, templates, minutes of meetings and other useful information. Staff can access the intranet any time they are logged onto the computer network. A key benefit of storing documentation on the intranet is that it can be updated easily and centrally, so that staff always have access to the most up-to-date version.

Cloud-based software

Cloud computing means storing data and programs on the internet, instead of your computer's hard drive, and accessing them from there. The cloud is simply a metaphor for the internet. Cloud-based software and storage means that individual users can access essential software applications and their documents from any computer that is linked to the internet. All software and documents produced using the software is stored by the cloud computing service provider on remote servers which are accessed via the internet.

This saves organisations time and effort downloading, installing and keeping software up to date. It also increases convenience, as users are able to access cloud resources from any device that can be connected to the internet and so can access their organisation's software and files from home.

Interactive whiteboards

This is a 'virtual' electronic version of a flip chart or whiteboard. It is typically used to lecture or give presentations and allows the user to write or draw over a presentation that is being projected onto the whiteboard. An interactive whiteboard is also touch-sensitive so just by touching the board with a finger the operator can open a new file or access information stored on a laptop. The biggest advantage of using an interactive whiteboard in a meeting is that all the relevant information can be saved electronically. For example, if a brainstorming session has taken place the notes can be easily saved, printed or e-mailed to participants later.

Audio conferencing

This is usually conducted by telephones on loud speaker, where a group of people sit around a telephone, communicating with other groups of people in other locations doing the same thing. One of the main drawbacks of holding a meeting in this way is that it is not always easy to identify the person speaking unless they give their name before talking. Another problem is that it is not possible to see the facial expressions or body language of those at other locations so it might be difficult to know how they really feel about something or what they really mean.

contd

Electronic diaries

These are particularly useful for setting up meetings as long as the Administrative Assistant has access to everyone's diary. The Administrative Assistant can look in the required e-diaries and check for a free date and time, so can arrange a meeting much more quickly. Once people have been invited to attend the meeting, the e-diaries will be updated automatically when the attendee accepts the invitation. Some e-diaries will also send reminders (a day or other specified time interval before the meeting) to the attendee's e-mail. The Administrative Assistant can use the e-diary to be reminded of key dates; for example when to chase confirmation of the room booking or when certain items need to be sent out. (Similarly, meetings can be cancelled in the same manner!)

Internet, network meetings and collaborative projects

Most organisations will either use a local area network (LAN), a wide area network (WAN) or the internet to connect computers, communicate, create/share resources and receive opinions and feedback from stakeholders.

Examples:

Instant messaging: a service provided to allow conversations in real time provided by many Internet Service Providers

Discussion (User) groups: allow the posting of messages which can then be read and answered. Usually for people interested in the same topics. Through use of passwords which only allow selected people to access these groups, the information contained in them can remain secure and confidential.

Webcams: digital cameras with special software attached to a computer, used to transfer images

Wikis: a collection of articles that users can add to and edit freely on line

Blogs: online diaries where thoughts or opinions can be displayed

Online collaboration forums are beneficial for tasks that require teamworking and are suited to the development of creative ideas or complex documents/projects.

They also offer opportunities for partnership working with customers, suppliers and other stakeholders who can view and comment on live documents/resources, as they are being developed.

Administrators may be given the task to set up and invite users to attend such a collaboration site. For example, they might create a Wiki or online discussion forum to allow customers, suppliers, employees, shareholders and other stakeholders to comment and share opinions on the organisation's products or services. This can provide valuable feedback and information to assist the organisation in improving its products or services and to increase customer satisfaction.

DON'T FORGET

Online collaborative forums create opportunities for stakeholders to share ideas and opinions.

ONLINE

For some great activities and case studies on the impact of new working practices, head to www.brightredbooks.net

ONLINE TEST

Head to www.brightredbooks.net and take the topic test.

THINGS TO DO AND THINK ABOUT

1   Outline how video conferencing, company intranets, e-mail and instant messaging support flexible working practices.

2   Explain what is meant by an online collaborative forum.

3   Outline the potential benefits to an organisation of setting up an online collaborative forum for all stakeholders.

4   What ICT equipment/resources are required to set up an online collaborative forum?

COMPUTER NETWORKS AND DATA-HANDLING

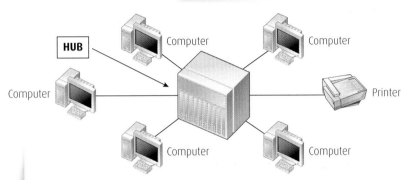

DON'T FORGET

LAN – computers linked within one building.
WAN – computers linked across different buildings anywhere in the world.

COMPUTER NETWORKS

Developments in ICT have undoubtedly improved workflow for organisations. The ability to access shared information, transmit information electronically and communicate around a computer network have all reduced the need for movement and duplication of documents. Networks allow computers to be linked to a server. A server is a very powerful computer where all of the files and software programs are stored. All the computers in the network can access these files. A **LAN** (local area network) links computers in the same workplace and a **WAN** (wide area network) links computers over a wider geographical area, for example linking company branches in Edinburgh and Glasgow.

Advantages of creating a network

- The organisation should save money as peripheral equipment can be shared. For example, every computer in the office will be networked to one printer.
- All users can access the same data and files. With good housekeeping, old files should be archived and no-one should be using out-of-date documents.
- Software can be shared and software licences for networks are cheaper than individual licences.
- Communication should also be more efficient as users can send messages by internal e-mail.
- The files may be more secure as passwords can be used for certain files and different users can be issued with different access rights, and this can be monitored by management.
- It is simpler to back up one large server than each individual computer.
- It is easier for management to monitor a network than individual computers.

Disadvantages of creating a network

- The initial costs of the equipment can be expensive and there are further costs involved in maintaining it.
- Staff will need to have expertise in managing a network.
- If the server suffers a technical fault, every computer in the firm will be affected. For example, a virus will spread through the entire network instead of affecting only one computer.
- It may also be easier for hackers to gain access to one main server rather than individual machines.
- Tight data security measures have to be put in place.

ONLINE

For a case study on computer networks, head to www.brightredbooks.net

VIDEO LINK

Head to www.brightredbooks.net and watch the video about software applications.

DATA HANDLING

Software applications – Summary

Most organisations will choose the software that suits their own business needs. The most common software applications used in business are shown in the following table.

contd

Word processing	This is a text processing system used to create various business documents such as letters, reports, minutes and forms. The main functions available include drawing tables, formatting text, creating electronic forms and mail merge. Word-processing software allows for speed and accuracy, the production of high-quality, easy-to-edit documents and integration with other software applications, such as databases and spreadsheets.
Spreadsheets	These are used to perform calculations and analyse numeric data. The main functions are performing calculations using simple and/or complex formulae, formatting cells to display values in currency or other formats and producing charts. Spreadsheets allow for accurate calculations, data to be updated if inputs are changed, data to be analysed using 'IF' and 'SUMIF' functions and charts to be used to help present and understand data.
Databases	These are used in the manner of an electronic filing system to store vast amounts of information about customers, suppliers or employees. The main functions are sorting data, performing queries and displaying data in reports. Information can be kept secure using access rights, information can be found quickly using criteria in queries, mail merge can be used to link information to other documents and data can be easily kept up-to-date and, when stored centrally, accessed by staff throughout the organisation.
Presentation software	This is used to present information on slides with supporting handouts. The main functions are the use of animation effects, sound and graphics to present information in a more interesting way. Presentation software can be used to gain the audience's attention – information can be integrated from other applications to support the presentation and presentations can be given a more professional look.

DON'T FORGET

The four most popular application packages are:
- word processing
- spreadsheet
- database
- presentation.

Most organisations will purchase a software application suite such as Microsoft Office. A suite merges different software with related functionality into a single package to provide economical software applications for individuals and organisations.

The advantages of using business software far outweigh any disadvantages. However, possible concerns when introducing new software to an organisation often include the cost of purchasing software, the time and expense of training staff, and the time and effort required to implement procedures to ensure data handling legislation is complied with.

ONLINE TEST

Test yourself on this topic at www.brightredbooks.net

 WHICH SOFTWARE WOULD YOU USE?

You are a Senior Administrative Assistant at Scott's Ltd, based in Dundee. You have been asked to complete the following tasks over the coming week. Copy the table below into your workbook and identify which data handling software you would use to undertake each of the following tasks (NB: WP = word processing; SS = spreadsheet; DB = database; PP = PowerPoint). The first one has been completed for you.

TASK	SOFTWARE			
	WP	SS	DB	PP
Send a memorandum to all staff	✓			
Create a graph showing quarterly sales figures				
Prepare budgets to record income and expenditure				
Create a presentation and handout on data-handling legislation to be issued to all staff				
Prepare a standard letter to be sent to 500 customers based in Glasgow				
Create a file of suppliers' details				
Calculate expenditure on office stationery				
Produce a staff policy document on health and safety in the workplace				
Prepare formal minutes following a meeting				
Prepare templates/business forms for staff				
Create a file for storing staff records and personal details				
Prepare a document showing total expenditure on employee remuneration – hours worked, rates of pay and total pay on a month-by-month basis for all employees				

THINGS TO DO AND THINK ABOUT

1 Describe the main difference between a local area network (LAN) and a wide area network (WAN).

2 Outline three advantages and three disadvantages of computer networks.

3 What is a computer software application suite?

FILE MANAGEMENT

VIDEO LINK

Watch the video about file management at www.brightredbooks.net

INTRODUCTION

File management is the organisation of computer files and is very important in any office. Organisations generally put their own procedures in place to ensure that files are stored properly. Procedures should cover the following:

File locations	Information should be given on where files should be stored, for example on the server, in which location and whether an external storage device is required. Some files will require to be password protected to limit access and to keep confidential information secure.
File names	Files should be stored in named folders with appropriate file names that will make it easy to find files. Users should also be able to recognise file extensions, for example .doc, .dbs, .xls and so on.
Routine maintenance	Information should be provided to staff about deleting unnecessary files as storage may need to be freed up on the server.
Back-up procedures	An important aspect of file management is ensuring that material is backed up. Back-up copies should be made regularly and staff should know the procedure for this. Some servers may automatically back up data on a regular basis.

BENEFITS OF GOOD FILE MANAGEMENT

Good file management:

- allows data to be shared by various users within an organisation
- allows data to be retrieved by various users within an organisation
- protects data to ensure accuracy and reliability
- ensures efficient workflow and time management

CONSEQUENCES OF POOR FILE MANAGEMENT

Poor file management can have the following consequences:

- Files may be lost, especially if the user does not know what the file is called.
- Time will be wasted looking for files, which can lead to stress for staff.
- Business can be lost, as customers and clients will be inconvenienced.
- Computer systems can slow down if the server is holding too many files.
- Wrong management decisions can be made if out-of-date information is used.
- There is the risk of a breach of data handling legislation.

Storage devices include servers, computer clouds, CD-ROMs, DVDs, MP3 files and USB/pen drives (also called memory sticks).

THE OVERALL IMPACT OF ICT ON WORKFLOW CAN HAVE THE FOLLOWING BENEFITS:

- a reduced need for movement of people: employees can access files from their desk
- fast communication around the organisation through the use of e-mail
- a reduced need to accommodate people in specific areas and increased opportunity for homeworking and teleworking
- more collaborative working by using online forums
- reduced costs from using hot desks and touchdown areas, as well as from sharing peripherals, for example printers
- fewer lost/misplaced files
- more efficient time/task management
- ability to reach customers all over the world and sell online 24/7

ONLINE TEST

Test yourself on this topic at www.brightredbooks.net

THINGS TO DO AND THINK ABOUT

Exam-style questions

1 Describe the ergonomic features that would ensure a good working environment. — 6 marks

2 Explain the impact of flexible working practices on organisations and individuals. — 6 marks

3 Describe ways in which networks can assist communication within an organisation. — 3 marks

4 Describe software applications that can be used in an organisation. — 6 marks

5 Explain how effective file management can be ensured within an organisation. — 4 marks

6 Justify an organisation's decision to change from an open-plan layout to a traditional cellular layout. — 4 marks

7 Outline four benefits of homeworking. — 4 marks

8 Other than homeworking, describe three flexible working practices. — 6 marks

9 Compare audio conferencing with video conferencing. — 2 marks

10 Describe the factors regarding IT that need to be considered for employees who want to start working from home. — 5 marks

11 Explain how flexible working practices can impact on an employee's well-being. — 4 marks

12 Creating a company intranet can be an expensive investment for an organisation. Justify this expense. — 2 marks

13 Outline the benefits of an organisation's decision to change from a traditional cellular office layout to an open-plan layout. — 4 marks

14 Establishing good practice in electronic file management is important for all organisations. Explain the benefits of this and the consequences of poor file management. — 6 marks

FEATURES OF GOOD CUSTOMER CARE

VIDEO LINK

Head to www.brightredbooks.net and watch the video on good customer service.

DON'T FORGET

A mission statement states an organisation's aims and objectives.

Example of a mission statement

'To be our customers' favourite place and way to eat and drink'

ONLINE

For more examples of mission statements, head to www.brightredbooks.net

DON'T FORGET

Without customers, there is no business!

DON'T FORGET

It is easier to retain existing customers than attract new ones.

DON'T FORGET

The Administrative Assistant has a key role to play in good customer service.

DON'T FORGET

It is better to under promise and over deliver!

DON'T FORGET

SLAs are contractual obligations

CUSTOMER SERVICE

To survive in today's competitive market modern business organisations must make a determined effort to provide the best possible service to their customers in the most cost-efficient way possible. Organisations usually produce a short **mission statement** which outlines their main aims and objectives.

The key features of good customer service are:

- putting the customer first
- communicating with customers effectively
- ensuring that staff are knowledgeable about products and services
- providing a good after-sales service
- dealing with complaints effectively and to the customer's satisfaction.

The role of the Administrative Assistant

When dealing with external customers, it is essential that the Administrative Assistant is aware of organisational policies and procedures and adheres to standards of service:

- **competence** – have a knowledge of the organisation's products or services
- **confidence** – smile, keep eye contact and display positive body language
- **concern** – listen attentively to what the customer has to say
- **courtesy** – be polite and don't argue with a customer even if they are shouting or being abusive
- **communication** – ask questions, take notes and keep the customer informed

CUSTOMER SERVICE POLICIES

Written customer care statement/strategy

This is a formal written statement about the standards that a customer can expect from an organisation. It is written to try to ensure that the customer gets what they want, at the right standard, quality and price. This statement should be shared with employees and customers so that everyone is aware of the standard expected. If a customer care strategy is properly implemented it will allow the organisation to benefit from:

- high levels of customer satisfaction
- increased sales
- greater customer loyalty
- a good reputation
- a higher level of competitiveness
- fewer complaints to deal with

Customer Service Level Agreement (SLA)

This is an agreement between the organisation and the customer describing what the organisation promises to be able to do and what the customer can expect. SLAs are contractual obligations.

An SLA opens communication between customer and supplier. It ensures responsibilities are documented and allows customers to know what to expect. For example, the following may be made clear in an SLA:

- delivery of products from the organisation to the customer incurs an additional charge
- installation of a product in the customer's home is not included in the purchase price
- delivery of products will take place within three working days from the day of purchase
- extended warranties on products incur an additional cost and must be purchased within one week of purchasing the product

SLAs allow organisations to set boundaries and expectations for both the supplier and the customer. The supplying organisation can clearly see where they have not met standards

contd

and where they have failed. The customer can also see where service has fallen short of expectations and might reasonably expect some compensation.

The main purpose of an SLA is to increase customer confidence and encourage the customer to continue to use the organisation; it also helps the organisation to establish standards against which they can evaluate their performance and compare with other organisations.

Staff are customers (internal customers)

Internal customers work within the company. For example, a company's IT department may provide a service to the other departments in the company. The IT department might therefore have an SLA with the other departments which states 'within one hour of notifying the IT department of a computer fault, we aim to have a technician with you to assess the fault'.

Complaints procedure

In reality, things go wrong and when they do it is important that a procedure is in place to deal with customer complaints and that both staff and customers know what this procedure is. Even though a customer has good reason to complain, as long as the complaint is handled effectively the organisation may not lose the customer. If the customer has a negative experience when making a complaint, the chances are they will tell others of their experience. The following should be covered by a complaints procedure:

- All complaints should be treated seriously and logged.
- They should be handled by specially trained staff.
- They should be acknowledged and the customer should be kept informed of what is happening.
- Time limits for dealing with complaints should be established. For example, all complaints will be dealt with within 10 working days.
- The result of the investigation into the complaint should be communicated to the customer promptly.

Some customers will accept bad service and not complain. However, they may simply not return to the organisation and will tell their friends and colleagues of their bad experience. This can impact on the organisation's reputation, sales and profits.

Reasons given by customers for not complaining include:

- 'It would take up too much time.'
- 'I don't want to make a fuss.'
- 'I don't know who to complain to.'
- 'I don't think it will make any difference.'

BENEFITS OF GOOD CUSTOMER SERVICE	EFFECTS OF POOR CUSTOMER SERVICE
Motivated and high-performing staff which is likely to increase productivity and ensure low staff turnover, as staff will want to work in an organisation where they are not continually facing customer complaints	Demotivated staff, low morale, poor working relationships and high rates of staff absenteeism and staff turnover. More staff required to deal with customer complaints
Satisfied and loyal customers who will offer repeat custom and recommend the organisation to family and friends	Dissatisfied customers who are unlikely to return and will not recommend the organisation to family and friends
Good reputation which will attract new customers	Increased complaints and poor reputation which is difficult to turn around
Increased sales revenue and profits for the organisation	Reduced sales revenue and profits for the organisation
Competitive edge in the marketplace	Decreased market share and greater need to spend money on advertising
Increased market share	Potential downfall of an organisation

DON'T FORGET

Remember the following!
- Survival depends on the customer.
- Repeat customers are important customers.
- Satisfaction is essential.
- Satisfaction depends on high quality.
- Satisfaction depends on continual improvement.

ONLINE TEST

Test your knowledge of customer service at www.brightredbooks.net

ONLINE

Head to www.brightredbooks.net to try out some case studies on customer care.

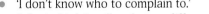

THINGS TO DO AND THINK ABOUT

1 What is the main purpose of a mission statement?
2 Explain the purpose of a customer care statement/strategy.
3 Explain the purpose of a service level agreement, giving an example of what could be included in such an agreement.
4 List four factors that should be included in a business's formal complaints procedure.
5 List some of the reasons that customers give for not making a formal complaint to a business organisation.

METHODS OF EVALUATING CUSTOMER CARE POLICY 1

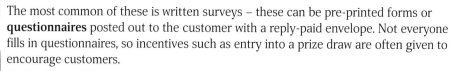

SURVEYING CUSTOMER SATISFACTION

It is important that organisations gain feedback on their customer care so that improvements can be made. Most organisations will use a variety of methods to do this.

Organisations who are willing to find and eliminate customers' problems achieve **customer focus**.

Organisations can ask for feedback to ensure that high standards of customer service are being met. This allows organisations to work on improving their customer service. There are various ways of collecting the information required, including:

- questionnaires
- comment cards
- telephone interviews
- interviews in the street
- online surveys

WRITTEN SURVEYS

The most common of these is written surveys – these can be pre-printed forms or **questionnaires** posted out to the customer with a reply-paid envelope. Not everyone fills in questionnaires, so incentives such as entry into a prize draw are often given to encourage customers.

Advantages of written surveys

- They give the customer the opportunity to comment and make them feel valued.
- They can be issued immediately after the customer has had dealings with the organisation and the experience is still fresh in the customer's mind.
- A permanent record is created which can be compared with previous surveys over a period of time.
- Results can be analysed and statistics extracted.

Disadvantages of written surveys

- The number of responses received is usually low and may not be representative of the whole customer base.
- The people who respond may only be those who are either very satisfied or very dissatisfied and the results may not therefore represent the full customer base
- They are not time-efficient. The survey has to be prepared, printed and sent out, and it may take some time for responses to be returned.
- The wording of questions is crucial. Questions should be pre-tested to ensure they are unambiguous, clear and understandable or customers will not bother to answer them.
- Many surveys are based on box ticking and so are not very flexible.
- Increasingly, **online surveys** are used as they are quick and simple to complete; however, people do not always read the questions properly, so the information provided may not be accurate.

TELEPHONE SURVEYS

Customers may be **telephoned** and asked pre-set questions. This can be cheaply and effectively outsourced to call centres, but some customers resent being interrupted at home.

Advantages of telephone surveys

- They make all those contacted feel valued.

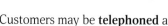

contd

- They generate instant data which can be used for fine-tuning customer service strategies.
- This kind of survey is cheap compared with other methods, particularly when it can be outsourced to a specialist call centre.
- Any ambiguous questions can be explained.

Disadvantages of telephone surveys

- Customers may resent being interrupted at work or at home.
- Customers may think there is a hidden agenda, such as the company trying to sell another product or service.
- Questions often have to be very simple when they are given only verbally. Complex questions cannot be used.
- If the organisation has outsourced the survey to a third party, the third party may lack the specialist knowledge to be able to explain the questions to the customer if the customer does not understand what is being asked.
- They may only reach certain groups of customers and so not be truly representative.

CUSTOMER FOCUS GROUPS

Customer **focus groups** are face-to-face meetings with a group of customers to allow them to provide immediate feedback to an organisation on its products and services. Being part of a focus group makes the customer feel valued and believe that the organisation will take their opinion into consideration. More detailed responses may be given from the customer as points are probed further than they are in surveys. However, a focus group can be expensive to arrange as a meeting venue will have to be paid for and the participants may have to be paid a nominal fee and have their travelling expenses reimbursed. Also, customers may only tell the organisation what they want to hear and not give any negative feedback.

Advantages of focus groups

- A pre-determined number of customers (which is representative of the customer base) can be invited to a focus group so you can guarantee the number of responses.
- The organisation gets instant feedback from a focus group.
- Those invited to a focus group will feel valued and are likely to give more positive responses than they might on a written survey.
- Customers may give more considered responses because everyone is given the opportunity to speak.
- Any questions which the customers do not understand can be clarified or re-worded.
- Additional questions can be asked to probe any issues which arise.

Disadvantages of focus groups

- There may be a time delay between the customer buying the product or service and the meeting of the focus group.
- All customers cannot be invited to the focus group so the organisation is sampling responses right from the start.
- The interaction of the individuals in the group may lead to an infectious negative experience and feedback.
- In order to get a national perspective, large companies would have to hold many focus groups throughout the country – an even more complicated, expensive and time-consuming exercise.

ONLINE

Head to www.brightredbooks.net to complete some great activities on customer care.

ONLINE TEST

Test yourself on this topic at www.brightredbooks.net

THINGS TO DO AND THINK ABOUT

1 Outline the different methods that may be used to survey customers' opinions.

2 Describe the advantages and disadvantages of setting up customer focus groups.

METHODS OF EVALUATING CUSTOMER CARE POLICY 2

FACE-TO-FACE INTERVIEWS

Face-to-face interviews may be deemed appropriate in some cases, especially where information is confidential; for example, if research is being done into financial services. Here, interviews are usually on a one-to-one basis, either at point of sale or later. Banks often make use of these.

Advantages of face-to-face interviews	Disadvantages of face-to-face interviews
• They are usually one-to-one interviews, allowing close interaction between interviewer and interviewee. • They allow for more private or personal questioning.	• They can be longer and more time-consuming. • They are less structured and it is therefore often more difficult to summarise what has been reported. • They are expensive, labour-intensive and fewer people are reached.

DON'T FORGET

Field research is gathered first hand through surveys. Desk research uses information that already exists.

MARKET RESEARCH

Market research is the process of collecting information and feedback about what customers think of an organisation and improvements that can be made. Market research is also used when organisations are thinking of launching new products to gain the opinion of potential customers prior to launch.

There are two main types of market research. The first is field or primary research, when information is collected from customers first hand through surveys and interviews.

The second is desk or secondary research, when an organisation uses information that already exists for the benefit of the business, government reports or information freely available on the internet.

MEMBERSHIP GROUPS

Membership groups usually grow out of some kind of brand loyalty; for example a particular product which is seen as having a cult following. To some extent members have already shown brand loyalty by joining the group.

Advantages of membership groups	Disadvantage of membership groups
• They are often formed for 'defensive' reasons: these groups often act as watchdogs or good ambassadors for a product (for example, Harley Davidson owners). • They create real brand loyalty. • Their activities may increase demand for the product.	• The one main disadvantage of membership groups is that feedback is biased in favour of the product.

MYSTERY SHOPPERS

To find out what the customers really experience, sometimes retail organisations will employ a **mystery shopper**. This is someone who is employed to act as a customer in order to experience the service and care ordinary shoppers receive. They will record their experiences and then feed back to the company either to praise or to reinforce any concerns regarding poor standards.

contd

Advantages of the mystery shopper	Disadvantages of the mystery shopper
• It gives a really clear idea of what a real customer might experience. • It is good for identifying staff training needs.	• It monitors and evaluates only the performance of the individual staff that the mystery shopper comes in contact with. • It normally only assesses front-line customer service. • There may be hostility from the staff.

SUGGESTION SCHEMES

Suggestion schemes are often used to encourage customers and employees to suggest new ideas.

Advantages of suggestion schemes	Disadvantages of suggestion schemes
• They are good for internal use, particularly if there is a reward attached, for example a voucher given for each suggestion adopted. • They work well with regular customers, for example in the hospitality/hotel industry, to ensure the organisation is providing what is required.	• The main disadvantage is that many customers ignore the opportunity to complete feedback slips and as a result feedback may focus only on very good or very poor customer service.

FREEPHONE LINES OR VIDEO BOOTH OPPORTUNITIES

A video booth provides the opportunity for a customer to make a video recording to give an organisation feedback on their shopping or other customer experience. A freephone number enables the customer to contact an organisation, free of charge, to provide feedback on their experience. They tend only to be used by customers who are reacting to very good or very poor customer service.

LOYALTY CARDS

Loyalty cards reward regular customers. When customers buy goods or services they gain points on their card which they can put towards the purchase of more goods and services. Rewards such as these are aimed at retaining customers by showing that the organisation values and cares about them. Furthermore, organisations use these cards to gather very valuable information on the spending habits of their customers, allowing them to alter prices and extend special offers.

THINGS TO DO AND THINK ABOUT

Exam-style questions

1 Describe the areas that might be covered by a customer service strategy. 6 marks

2 Describe the importance of good customer service to an organisation. 6 marks

3 Describe the consequences, and their implications, of poor customer service. 6 marks

4 Compare a mystery shopper with a customer focus group. 2 marks

5 Outline four reasons given by customers for not complaining. 4 marks

6 Justify the need for a complaints policy. 2 marks

7 Outline the qualities required by an Administrative Assistant that would ensure effective customer care. 4 marks

 ONLINE

Head to www.brightredbooks.net to complete some great activities on customer care.

 ONLINE TEST

Test yourself on this topic at www.brightredbooks.net

METHODS OF EVALUATING CUSTOMER CARE POLICY 3

E-COMMERCE

One major area of business where IT is dramatically impacting on the way organisations operate and employees work (particularly sales staff) is e-commerce.

E-commerce can be defined as buying and selling goods/services over the internet. You can sell all sorts of things online – clothes, music, holidays, furniture, second-hand items, specially designed items and so on.

Effective e-commerce can contribute to effective customer care in a number of ways:

- A wide range of customers can be catered for worldwide through the company's website.
- Selling online can reduce business costs and allow customers to enjoy lower prices.
- Companies are able to respond quickly to customer orders. An online order can be executed much more quickly than traditional ordering methods.
- The company can monitor what customers are buying and use this information for marketing purposes.

DON'T FORGET

Online customers will expect the same high standard of service as those visiting the organisation in person.

TOTAL QUALITY MANAGEMENT

Total quality management (TQM) is a concept that acknowledges that all employees in an organisation have individual as well as collective responsibility for maintaining high standards of quality. The fundamental principle of TQM is: get it right, first time and every time. The relationship between improving quality and developing the business has been demonstrated again and again (especially by the Japanese electronics industry).

TQM involves setting and monitoring standards, meeting targets and delivering what has been promised by a courteous and helpful staff. It also allows organisations to measure themselves against other organisations, a process sometimes known as **benchmarking**.

For TQM to be successful, quality has to be clearly defined and it must be measurable, and the commitment of all staff is essential.

The following activities are all highly recommended for successful TQM.

- Listen to what customers say – share feedback with everyone in the company.
- Create a 'Best Customer Service Awards' board to publicly recognise staff members who have provided particularly excellent customer service.
- Provide special customer service training.
- Create an internal newsletter that shares good practice around the whole organisation.
- Provide warranties, guarantees and refunds.

DON'T FORGET

TQM requires the commitment of all staff.

🔧 ACTIVITY QUICK QUESTIONS

1 Explain the difference between desk and field research.
2 What is the purpose of a mystery shopper?
3 Explain what is meant by Total Quality Management.
4 Explain what is meant by an internal customer.

CASE STUDY

McDonald's prides itself on delivering only the highest levels of quality, service and cleanliness to all of its customers. The key to our continued success is continually monitoring and acting on the feedback given to us by our customers. We strive to be a progressive market leader and we can only stay ahead of the rest by listening to the most important ambassadors of our brand – our customers!

The importance of customer service

We have recognised that complaints, enquiries or positive feedback from customers are precious pieces of information. When used properly complaints can help us fine-tune our business and meet our customers' needs. Equally important is to hear and effectively manage complaints from customers. If the company is not seen to be dealing with poor experiences then disgruntled customers will vote with their feet and we will lose their business.

Do you know that only 5 per cent of customers with a complaint ever put their complaint to a customer services department? A further 45 per cent of customers with a complaint take time to raise their concerns on the spot and speak with an employee. We need to ensure that, for such customers, their complaint is resolved satisfactorily there and then. If this is not achieved, we run the risk that these customers will not voice their concerns in the future, thereby losing for us an opportunity to gather important customer feedback. The remaining 50 per cent of customers who encounter a problem don't make a complaint. In order to move towards a situation where this 50 per cent are more likely to voice their concerns, we encourage both the Customer Services department and restaurant employees to be accessible to our customers and open to feedback. Each restaurant should display a name plaque indicating the Shift Running Manager's name. In addition, each manager should wear a name badge displaying their first name. The customer care employee should ensure that, as the first point of contact for customers, they are welcoming and accessible at all times. Finally, the restaurant's telephone number should be on display. Combined, these initiatives should help to create an inviting and customer-friendly environment. It is imperative that we encourage our customers to voice their concerns within the restaurant itself so our restaurant management have the opportunity to resolve the problem then and there.

Employee training

A very important part of our department's remit is working with restaurant employees to give them the tools and resources they need to deal with complaints effectively. We teach them how to deal with all types of customer feedback: for example a basic nutritional enquiry or a service issue. Most importantly, we encourage our employees to recognise a dissatisfied customer and diffuse potential complaints.

Questions

1. What does McDonald's see as the key to their continued success?
2. According to the article, what will customers do if they feel that their complaint has not been adequately dealt with?
3. What percentage of unhappy customers never raise a complaint?
4. What strategies has McDonald's used to try and create a customer friendly environment?
5. Outline some of the training techniques that new staff undertake and explain why you think McDonald's trains its employees to handle complaints.

 THINGS TO DO AND THINK ABOUT

Exam-style questions

1	Describe the methods a company may use to gather information about customer satisfaction.	6 marks
2	Describe good practice an organisation could adopt to ensure that complaints are handled effectively.	6 marks
3	Justify the cost of providing training in customer care to an Administrative Assistant.	2 marks
4	Justify the importance of a mission statement to an organisation.	2 marks
5	Justify the need for a complaints policy.	2 marks

 ONLINE

Head to www.brightredbooks.net to complete some great activities on customer care.

 ONLINE TEST

Test yourself on this topic at www.brightredbooks.net

 DON'T FORGET

To go online to try the specimen exam paper.

INDEX

3D cell references 80

Access 17, 35, 85–6
action plans 94
Administrative Assistant 88, 120
animations 10–11
applications, working between 85–7

breaks 56–7
bulleted lists 44–5
business letters 36–7

career breaks 111
cell references 64, 80
cells, named 65
charts 80–2
cloud-based software 114
comments
    in documents 61
    in spreadsheet 84–5
communication 6–15, 113–15
    barriers to 7
    electronic 14–15, 113–15
    methods 6
    software 8–13
conditional formatting 75
conditional formulae 71–3
conferencing 114
conflict 99
contracts, work 110
customer care 120–7

data handling 116–17
    legislation 106–7
databases 16–35
    integration 34–5
    relational 16–19
    see also Access; forms; queries; reports
delegation 90
document views 42

e-commerce 126
e-mail 14–15, 113
electronic diaries 95, 115
electronic forms 51
endnotes 61
ergonomics 108–9
Excel, copying data from/into 12, 51, 71, 85–6

file management 118–19
filtering, of spreadsheet data 76–7
find and replace 63
flexible working practices 109, 110, 112
focus groups 123
footers 58–9
footnotes 61
formatting marks, displaying 42–3
formatting text 43
forms 16, 20–3, 51
    creating 20
    editing layout 22–3
    printing 23
    viewing data 21
functions 66–7

Gantt charts 93
Glow 14
grammar 62–3
grouping, of data 78

handouts 13
headers 58–9
headings 52
health and safety 102–5
horizontal lookups 68–71
hyperlinks 11

IF statements 73
    nested 74
indents 46
internet 115
interviews 124
intranet 114
itineraries 37

leadership 100–1
line spacing 44
lookups 68–71
loyalty cards 125

mail merge 40–1
mailing labels 34, 41
margins 55
market research 124
meetings documentation 38–9
mobile phones 113
monitoring progress 97
mystery shoppers 124

networks, computer 116
number formats 45
numbered lists 44–5

objects, linking 35
office layout 108
outlining 78
Outlook 14–15

page orientation 55
paragraph spacing 44
personal development plans 94–5
pivot charts 84
pivot tables 82–3
planning aids 92–4
PowerPoint 8
    copying from Access 35
    importing data from Excel 12
presentation software 8–13
presentations
    editing 8–9
    importing data 12
    printing 13
    views 8–9
primary keys 17, 18
priorities 93, 96

queries 16, 19, 24–7
    aggregate 27
    calculated 26–7
    copying from 35
    creating 24
    criteria 25

exporting from 35
quick access toolbar 43

ranges of cells 65
relational databases 16–19
relationships 17–19
reports 16, 28–33
    adding graphics 31
    calculations in 32–3
    editing 30–1
    exporting from 35
    steps in creating 28–9
    tidying up 30

skills, team members' 100
slides
    animations 10–11
    backgrounds 10
SMART targets 92
sorting
    in design view 31
    of spreadsheet data 76
spelling 62–3
spreadsheets 64–87
    printing 87
    see also Excel
styles 52–3
suggestion schemes 125
summaries, of numeric values 32–3
surveys 122–3

tables 16, 48–51
    calculations in 51
    converting to/from text 50
    creating 48–9
    exporting/copying from 35, 86
    inserting data from Excel 51
    selecting items 49
    sorting in 50
tables of contents 54
tabs 46–7
targets, setting 92–5
teams 98–101
templates 36
thesaurus 63
time stealers 90
time and task management 89–91
to-do lists 94
total quality management (TQM) 126
totals queries 27
transitions 11

vertical lookups 68–9

watermarks 60
Word, copying to/from 86–7
word count 62
word processing 36–63
    see also Word
working hours 110
working practices 108–15
workplace regulations 102–27
worksheets, multiple 79

zooming 43

128